NONPERFORMING LOANS WATCH IN ASIA 2025

ASIAN DEVELOPMENT BANK

ADB

6 ADB Avenue, Mandaluyong City, 1550 Metro Manila, Philippines
Tel +63 2 8632 4444; Fax +63 2 8636 2444
www.adb.org

ISBN 978-92-9277-396-0 (print); 978-92-9277-397-7 (PDF); 978-92-9277-398-4 (ebook)
Publication Stock No. TCS250316-2
DOI: http://dx.doi.org/10.22617/TCS250316-2

Notes:
In this publication, "$" refers to United States dollars and "CNY" refers to yuan.
ADB recognizes "China" as the People's Republic of China; "Hong Kong" as Hong Kong, China; "Korea" and "South Korea" as the Republic of Korea; and "Vietnam" as Viet Nam.

Cover design by Michael Cortes.

Contents

Tables and Figures iv

Acknowledgments v

Abbreviations vi

Glossary vii

Executive Summary viii

1 **Introduction: Asia's Nonperforming Loans Market** 1

2 **Nonperforming Loans in Asia: 2024 Data Analysis** 6

3 **Asset Management Companies Nonperforming Loans Transaction Trends in the Region** 11

4 **Impediments to Nonperforming Loans Transactions in the Region** 18

5 **Credit Servicers in the Region** 23

6 **Credit Risks and Nonperforming Loan Forecasts** 25

7 **Case Study of the People's Republic of China** 31

8 **Case Study of the Republic of Korea** 35

9 **Case Study of Viet Nam** 38

10 **Conclusion** 41

Annexes

1 International Public Asset Management Companies Forum 42

2 Nonperforming Loans in Asia and Europe—Causes, Impacts, and Resolution Strategies 45

3 Practical Insights from the ADB 2024 Report on Nonperforming Loan Trading Platforms in Asia 46

4 The European Union Best-Execution Guidelines—Lessons Learned Relevant for Asian Nonperforming Loans Markets 47

5 Forecasting Nonperforming Loan Ratio and Identifying Key Determinants in International Public Asset Management Companies Forum Countries Using Deep Learning 49

6 2024 People's Republic of China Nonperforming Loans Markets and Index Reports 57

Bibliography 58

Tables and Figures

Tables

1 Key Nonperforming Loans Metrics 7

2 Summary of Forecast Accuracy and Key Determinants of Nonperforming Loan Ratios 29

Figures

1 Nonperforming Loans Volume ($ billion) with Nonperforming Loans Ratio (%) by Region and Subregion 8

2 International Public Asset Management Companies Forum Question—Recent Nonperforming Loans Transaction Activity, Current/Past 12 Months 13

3 International Public Asset Management Companies Forum Question—Estimated Total Nonperforming Loans Transactions in Your Jurisdiction in the Last 12 Months 13

4 International Public Asset Management Companies Forum Question—Volume of Nonperforming Loans Sales Performed by Your Asset Management Companies in 2024 14

5 International Public Asset Management Companies Forum Question—Who Banks Can Sell NPLs To 15

6 International Public Asset Management Companies Forum Question—Types of Nonperforming Loans Buyers Most Active in Your Market 15

7 International Public Asset Management Companies Forum Question—Most Frequent Nonperforming Loans Transactions in Your Country 16

8 International Public Asset Management Companies Forum Question—Most Common Sectors for Nonperforming Loans Transactions in Past 12 Months 16

9 International Public Asset Management Companies Forum Question—Asset Management Companies Nonperforming Loans Portfolio Composition 17

10 International Public Asset Management Companies Forum Question—Key Impediments to Nonperforming Loans Transactions Faced by Your Country 19

11 International Public Asset Management Companies Forum Question—Maturity of Nonperforming Loans Transactions Market in Your Country 24

12 International Public Asset Management Companies Forum Question—Maturity of Your Country's Nonperforming Loans Servicers 24

13 International Public Asset Management Companies Forum Question—Credit Risk Deterioration by Industry (Lending Area) in the Next 24 Months 26

14 International Public Asset Management Companies Forum Question—Expected Rise in Nonperforming Loans by Sector in Next 2 Years 27

15 International Public Asset Management Companies Forum Question—Expected Nonperforming Loans Volumes in 2026 Compared to Current Levels 27

16 Nonperforming Loan Ratio Projections for the Next 4 Quarters 28

Acknowledgments

Nonperforming Loans (NPL) Watch in Asia 2025 is part of the initiatives of the Asian Development Bank (ADB) and the International Public Asset Management Companies Forum (IPAF) toward strengthening Asia's financial safety net and crisis response and resolution mechanisms. This report is produced with support from TA 10180: Asia's Financial Safety Net, Resolution Mechanisms, and Financial Integration and Resilience, financed by ADB's technical assistance special fund and the Republic of Korea e-Asia and Knowledge Partnership Fund.

This inaugural edition of NPL Watch in Asia was prepared by a team from ADB's Economic Research and Development Impact Department under the supervision of Jong Woo Kang, director of the Regional Cooperation and Integration Division.

The production of NPL Watch Asia was led by Inha Shin (regional cooperation specialist) and Eric Cloutier (consultant, group head of Banking Regulations and head of the Global FS Regulatory Centre at Forvis Mazars), with support from the ADB–IPAF team comprising Alexander Raabe (economist), Paulo Rodelio M. Halili (principal economics officer), Angel Love Roque (operations analyst), and Lilibeth C. Perez (consultant). Michael Cortes created the cover design. Edith Creus implemented the typesetting and layout. Maria Guia de Guzman proofread the report. Paulo Rodelio M. Halili and Carol Ongchangco assisted in proofreading and page proof checking. Eric Van Zant edited the manuscript.

Contributions from Youngwoo Jeong (senior manager, Korea Asset Management Corporation) and Congyi Hu (associate, Zhejiang Zheshang Asset Management Co., Ltd.) are gratefully acknowledged.

Abbreviations

ADB	Asian Development Bank
AMC	asset management company
PRC	People's Republic of China
DATC	Viet Nam Debt and Asset Trading Corporation
IMF	International Monetary Fund
IPAF	International Public AMCs Forum
KAMCO	Korea Asset Management Corporation
MAMCO	Mongolia Asset Management Corporation
MSME	micro, small, and medium-sized enterprise
NPL	nonperforming loan
PPA	PT Perusahaan Pengelola Aset
RAMCO	Recovered Asset Management Company
SAM	Sukhumvit Asset Management Co., Ltd.
SME	small and medium-sized enterprise
VAMC	Viet Nam Asset Management Company
ZSAMC	Zhejiang Zheshang Asset Management Company

Glossary

NPL volume (or gross NPLs): NPLs are defined and reported differently from country to country, as there is no international standard. For countries reporting Financial Soundness Indicators (FSI) to the International Monetary Fund, the FSI Compilation Guide recommends reporting NPLs when: (i) payments of principal and interest are past due by 90 days or more; (ii) interest payments equal to 90 days' interest or more have been capitalized, refinanced, or rolled over; and (iii) loans are less than 90 days past due, but recognized as nonperforming under national supervisory guidance.

NPL ratio: NPL volume divided by the total gross value of the loan portfolio (including gross NPLs before the deduction of specific loan loss provisions).

NPL coverage ratio: Total specific loan loss provisions divided by gross NPLs.

Net NPLs: NPLs minus specific loan loss provisions.

- Net NPL ratio: Net NPLs divided by the total gross value of the loan portfolio (including gross NPLs before the deduction of specific loan loss provisions).
- Net NPL/capital: Net NPLs divided by capital. Capital is measured as capital plus reserves; for cross-border consolidated data, total regulatory capital can also be used.

Market share NPLs: Total country gross NPLs divided by total region gross NPLs.

Market share loans: Total country gross loans divided by total region gross loans.

Executive Summary

Nonperforming Loans (NPL) Watch in Asia 2025 is a joint initiative of the Asian Development Bank (ADB) and the International Public Asset Management Companies Forum (IPAF) to monitor NPL trends and resolution efforts across Asia. This first edition establishes a new annual report, supporting policy alignment and market development.

A New Annual Report to Support Coordinated, Data-Driven Nonperforming Loans Resolution Across Asia

The report responds to a 2024 IPAF Summit mandate to strengthen regional coordination through structured insights and shared diagnostics. IPAF brings together 18 members across 8 countries to promote market development, capacity building, and policy dialogue. With ADB support, it fosters regionally grounded approaches to financial stability.

The report draws on

- a 2025 survey of IPAF members covering, among others, impediments to NPL resolution and sales, transactions activity, servicing capacity, and credit risks and the NPL outlook.
- interviews with asset management companies (AMCs) in three major contributing countries for this report, the People's Republic of China (PRC), the Republic of Korea, and Viet Nam.
- research and existing literature, including ADB (2021), a study on NPL resolution frameworks in Asia and Europe and the 2024 ADB report on NPL transaction platforms.

Key Insights

- **Asia continues to demonstrate resilience to NPLs:** NPL ratios continued edging lower in 2024 (to 1.6% vs 1.7% in 2023). NPL volumes decreased only slightly over the same period (by $13.2 billion year on year, reaching $700.19 billion in 2024).
- **Signs of credit stress are accelerating in some sectors:** Growing pressure is observed in real estate, small and medium-sized enterprises, and retail credit. NPL growth is expected through 2027, concentrated in construction, consumer finance, and some state-owned enterprises. Risk remains sectoral rather than systemic. Capacity to respond in the region is uneven.
- **Structural barriers continue to limit market development:** Pricing gaps, restricted domestic and foreign investor access, weak enforcement, fragmented data, and regulatory friction continue to stall transactions.

- **Diverging national approaches to AMC reform:** The PRC is scaling decentralized AMCs. The Korea Asset Management Corporation sets the regional benchmark for the resolution and management of NPLs and the use of digital servicing platforms. And Viet Nam's dual AMC model is progressing through restructuring and platform expansion.
- **AMCs remain central but under growing operational pressure:** AMCs lead most of the transactions in the region. The PRC and the Republic of Korea are scaling portfolio sales; Viet Nam remains largely bilateral, with real estate and corporate debt concentration.
- **Digital servicing platforms are emerging but need scaling:** The Republic of Korea's *OnBid* is the most advanced. Viet Nam's portal enhances visibility, but execution remains limited. Digitalization elsewhere is still in its early stage. For example, PRC actively uses private bidding platforms—such as Taobao—which differs from the public, NPL-focused models used in the Republic of Korea and Viet Nam).

1 Introduction: Asia's Nonperforming Loans Market

East Asia and Southeast Asia remain relatively stable through regulatory measures and asset management companies (AMCs), though sector-specific vulnerabilities persist. South Asia and Central Asia face slower NPL resolution due to structural challenges and limited market-based tools.

Background: The Impacts of the Asian Financial Crisis and Global Financial Crisis

The nonperforming loans (NPL) landscape in Asia during 2024 and 2025 reflects a complex interplay of economic conditions, sector vulnerabilities, and regulatory responses across various subregions. While East Asia and Southeast Asia have effectively maintained relatively lower NPL ratios due to stringent regulatory environments, proactive policy interventions, and robust economic performance, regions such as South Asia and Central Asia continue to grapple with higher and more persistent NPL ratios, largely influenced by structural impediments, broader economic instabilities, and commodity dependence in some countries (e.g., Nepal, Pakistan, and Sri Lanka).

Historically, two significant economic crises—the Asian financial crisis of 1997–1998 and the global financial crisis of 2008–2009—substantially reshaped NPL dynamics within the region. During the Asian crisis, NPLs increased sharply in East Asia and Southeast Asian economies, with countries like Indonesia and Thailand reaching ratios of over 40%. This spike was driven by rapid credit expansion, lax lending standards, and abrupt currency depreciation. The subsequent policy responses, including the establishment of asset management companies (AMCs), finance sector restructuring, and macroprudential tightening, were pivotal in reducing these ratios over the following decade.

The global financial crisis had a pronounced impact on Central Asian economies, primarily due to their dependence on global commodity markets and external financing. NPL ratios linked directly to declines in global commodity prices and subsequent economic downturns increased considerably in countries such as Kazakhstan and Tajikistan.

Postcrisis Recovery and Current Nonperforming Loans Situation

Asia's NPL resilience is growing—but recovery capacity and market depth remain uneven. Postcrisis recovery dynamics have been occurring at different speeds across Asia's subregions.

While efforts to manage the NPL challenges through regulatory adjustments and the creation of AMCs had positive results in many jurisdictions, structural weaknesses in judicial processes, insufficient market infrastructure, and limited foreign investor participation have slowed recovery for some countries.

East Asia

Postcrisis recovery in East Asia has been shaped by relatively strong regulatory capacity and more conservative risk-taking by banks. Several jurisdictions benefited from lessons learned during previous financial crises, which translated into cautious credit allocation, timely interventions, and the sustained presence of AMCs. Nonetheless, the pace of recovery across sectors remains uneven, particularly in real estate-related exposures and smaller corporate segments. Efforts to improve insolvency resolution and support secondary markets are ongoing, with regulators increasingly focused on strengthening institutional frameworks to support long-term resilience.

South Asia

In South Asia, economic recovery has progressed gradually, reflecting persistent structural challenges in the banking sector. While regulatory responses have improved, including enhancements to insolvency frameworks and recapitalization efforts, the depth of NPL resolution tools remains limited. The exposure of banks to micro, small, and medium-sized enterprises and sectors affected by inflationary pressures has added to asset quality concerns. Although headline NPL ratios remain relatively stable, with only minimal increases observed, they remain comparatively high at 3.6% for the subregion in 2024 (compared to Asia's average of 1.6%). This underlines remaining vulnerabilities, particularly in jurisdictions where public sector banks dominate and market-based resolution mechanisms are to be developed.

Southeast Asia

Southeast Asia's financial systems have remained broadly stable, aided by regulatory forbearance and targeted support measures. While these measures helped avert a near-term deterioration in asset quality, they also deferred recognition of stress in micro, small, and medium-sized enterprises; consumer finance; and real estate. As support schemes are phased out, regulators are focusing on strengthening early warning systems, promoting debt restructuring tools, and exploring market-based resolution channels. Some jurisdictions have initiated efforts to establish specialized platforms and broaden the investor base for distressed assets to reinforce long-term resolution capacity.

Central Asia

While NPL ratios remain slightly elevated on average, at 2.7% for 2024, they continue to trend downward (-0.1% in 2024, from 2.8% in 2023) as postcrisis recovery progresses, supported in part by public sector-led resolution initiatives. Several jurisdictions have established asset management entities or similar mechanisms to address banking sector fragilities. However, the operationalization of these frameworks has faced challenges, including limited investor participation, underdeveloped legal infrastructure, and thin capital markets. While improvements have been recorded in regulatory oversight and bank supervision, continued progress will depend on broader institutional strengthening and greater regional coordination in financial sector reform.

Contribution of Transactions Platforms for Nonperforming Loans Resolution in the Region

Technological advancements and digital innovations provide new avenues for more efficient NPL management and resolution. For example, the Korea Asset Management Corporation's (KAMCO) innovative transaction platform represents a pivotal advancement in the management of NPLs in the Republic of Korea. This platform is designed to facilitate the buying and selling of distressed assets, making the process more transparent and efficient.

Leveraging its experience, KAMCO has worked with other International Public AMCs Forum (IPAF) members over the years to help promote the development of similar transaction platforms in the region, as discussed in the latest May 2024 Asian Development Bank report on How to Build Nonperforming Loan Trading Platforms in Asia and the Pacific (ADB 2024a).

For example, KAMCO advised the Viet Nam Asset Management Company (VAMC) on revamping its online platform to serve as an information hub where buyers and sellers can seek relevant NPL data and thus support investors. The platform was established in October 2021 and has played a significant role in increasing transactions in the country, making the market more active and mature.

Challenges persist in creating a pan-Asian transaction platform, such as differences in legal and regulatory frameworks and gaps in data quality and valuation standards. In this context, country- or region-specific modular platforms—featuring secure data rooms and auction tools—are seen as the most realistic and pragmatic solution in the near term. Over time, these localized platforms could potentially be integrated into a central hub, once foundational systems are firmly in place.

Additionally, increasing adoption of financial technology, including blockchain-based solutions for transaction transparency and big data analytics for loan assessment, offer promising strategies for overcoming existing impediments such as information asymmetry and inefficiencies in loan resolution processes.

Nonperforming Loans Transaction Market in the Region: Importance of Asset Management Companies

AMCs continue to play a critical role in shaping Asia's evolving NPL transaction markets. Across the region, public AMCs also remain central to resolution—but transaction scale, structure, and tools vary widely.

AMCs not only act as resolution agents for distressed assets but also as market enablers—facilitating price discovery, improving transparency, and expanding investor participation. Their mandate has grown beyond simple NPLs and asset warehousing to include platform development, legal reform support, and cross-border coordination.

Recent developments underline their strategic importance. For example, in the Republic of Korea, KAMCO has emerged as a regional reference point, facilitating both domestic and transactions through digital tools and structured sales mechanisms. Several other economies, including the People's Republic of China (PRC) and Viet Nam, have similarly relied on AMCs to stabilize asset prices and ensure orderly transactions in both primary and secondary NPL markets. Notably, the PRC's national AMCs and regional AMCs (such as Zhejiang Zheshang Asset Management Company [ZSAMC] and Tianjin Binhai Zhengxin Asset Management Company) have significantly deepened market liquidity. Meanwhile, in Southeast Asia, institutions such as the VAMC and the Viet Nam Debt and Asset Trading Corporation (DATC) in Viet Nam are gradually expanding secondary market activity.

The IPAF has strengthened this ecosystem. Its coordination on topics such as securitization frameworks, digital trading platforms, and AMC governance has enhanced regional capacity to manage NPLs. And its technical cooperation with ADB continues to reduce entry barriers for private and international investors.

Going forward, AMCs are expected to remain central to both stabilizing financial systems and building the architecture of transparent, investable NPL markets across Asia.

Nonperforming Loans Servicers Remain Mostly Local Companies

The development of a robust NPL servicing industry remains uneven across Asia, with most markets still reliant on local, often small-scale operators. While domestic firms play an important role in bridging cultural, legal, and language complexities, the servicing sector overall remains fragmented and underdeveloped relative to the scale and potential of regional NPL markets.[1]

Survey responses from IPAF members indicate that in most jurisdictions, third-party servicing remains limited and is often concentrated among a few local providers. Interview feedback also points to constraints in servicing capacity, particularly in handling large or complex portfolios. Cross-border activity is rare, and international players remain largely absent due to regulatory barriers and market size considerations. As transaction activity expands—particularly in retail and small and medium-sized enterprise (SME) segments—these structural limitations could impede timely resolution and investor participation.

Public AMCs in several jurisdictions have partially filled servicing gaps by taking on key functions such as borrower engagement, collateral management, and enforcement coordination. In markets like the Republic of Korea and Viet Nam, AMCs have also helped set operational benchmarks and provided informal training grounds for servicing talent.

Public AMCs continue to fill some of these gaps, especially in markets where private servicers are nascent or unable to handle scale. Strengthening the servicing industry will be essential to support the evolution of efficient and scalable NPL markets in Asia.

Significant Impediments Remain

While progress is evident, several structural and operational frictions continue to shape the development trajectory of NPL markets across Asia. Survey results indicate that information asymmetry and data quality remain top concerns for market participants, with investors often citing limited access to granular loan-level details and valuation methodologies. Legal and regulatory inconsistencies—especially around enforcement and asset recovery—complicate the investment landscape, particularly for cross-border transactions.

Market infrastructure also presents a mixed picture. Although digital platforms and AMC-facilitated transactions are gaining traction, secondary markets remain relatively shallow. Restrictions on private investor participation in certain jurisdictions and limited standardization of transaction processes were also highlighted in consultations. Strengthening legal clarity, improving data transparency, and deepening secondary markets will be critical to unlocking greater capital participation and supporting a more resilient regional NPL ecosystem.

The next section details the impediments.

[1] NPL servicers are specialized firms or units responsible for managing, collecting, and resolving NPLs on behalf of creditors or asset owners, such as banks, AMCs, or investors. Their key roles include debt collection and restructuring, asset recovery and liquidation, borrower negotiation, and legal enforcement.

Looking Forward: Nonperforming Loans Amid Heightened Uncertainty

Asia's NPL market has seen remarkable progress in recent years. Current NPL levels are significantly lower and relatively stable across most jurisdictions. However, it remains crucial to monitor developments closely and prepare for potential downside scenarios. Progress has been uneven across countries, underscoring the need for tailored approaches to NPL management.

Looking ahead, the regional NPL landscape faces renewed pressure from global economic uncertainties, geopolitical tensions, and sector-specific vulnerabilities—particularly in real estate, infrastructure, and manufacturing. A prolonged global slowdown, exacerbated by trade disputes and geopolitical conflicts, could trigger new waves of NPLs, especially in highly leveraged corporate sectors and economies reliant on external trade and commodity exports.

To navigate these challenges, strong regulatory frameworks, efficient market structures, and proactive policy interventions will be essential. Continued efforts to enhance judicial efficiency, improve market transparency, and foster investor participation will be key to developing a more effective and integrated secondary NPL market across Asia.

2 Nonperforming Loans in Asia: 2024 Data Analysis

In 2024, the total volume of NPLs across Asia reached approximately $700.19 billion, down marginally from $713.34 billion in 2023 (about 1.8% points) to a broadly stable credit environment across the region (Table 1). However, the aggregate figure masks notable variation across subregions. East Asia remained the dominant contributor, led by the PRC and Japan, while South Asia and Central Asia recorded more pronounced increases, partly driven by loan book expansion. In contrast, NPL volumes declined overall in Southeast Asia, with improvements in Malaysia and Singapore offsetting pressures in Cambodia and Viet Nam.

Despite rising volumes in some markets, most economies maintained stable or improving NPL ratios, though persistent stress in countries like Bangladesh, Sri Lanka, and Viet Nam highlights the need for targeted reforms and stronger resolution frameworks.

Important note: *Due to data limitations, not all economies within the region and subregions could be included. As a result, this report and its analysis focus on the larger economies only—specifically those with a reported gross NPL stock exceeding $250 million as of 31 December 2024. Consequently, the total and subtotal figures presented are illustrative estimates, intended for discussion purposes only.*

Five-Year Context

Over the past 5 years, Asia's NPL landscape has evolved significantly. NPLs rose temporarily in the pandemic shock in 2020 across many economies, particularly lower-income countries. However, from 2021 onward, a combination of regulatory forbearance, targeted fiscal support, and economic recovery helped stabilize asset quality. By 2024, several economies had returned to or improved upon their pre-pandemic NPL ratios, although vulnerabilities remain in certain sectors and jurisdictions (Figure 1).

East Asia

East Asia holds the largest volume of NPLs in the region, contributing $520.34 billion (74.3%) of Asia's total. But NPL volume remained stable, decreasing a marginal $5.1 billion (1.0 percentage point) from 2024. Similarly, the average NPL ratio on the other hand slightly decreased, reaching 1.4% in 2024 (from 1.5% in 2024). This follows a consistent downward trend from 2020 (Table 1).

Within this subregion, the PRC remains the largest single contributor, with $449.2 billion in NPLs, down slightly from $454.3 billion in 2023. The PRC accounts for 62.5% of the regional total (or 86.3% of East Asia's NPLs), mainly due to the sheer volume of its banking sector.

Table 1: Key Nonperforming Loans Metrics

Banking Sector NPL Volume and Ratio in Asia Over the Past 5 years (as % of gross loans)															
		NPL Volume							NPL Ratio						
		Latest 2024			Latest 2023	Variation			Over the past 5 years					Variation	
		($ bln)	% sugroup	% total	($ bln)	($ bln)	2024–2023Δ (%)		2020	2021	2022	2023	2024	2024–2023Δ (pp)	
Asia		**700.19**		**100.0%**	**713.34**	**-13.2**	**-1.8%**	▼				**1.7%**	**1.6%**	**-0.1%**	▼
East Asia		**520.34**	**100.0%**	**74.3%**	**525.43**	**-5.1**	**-1.0%**	▼				**1.5%**	**1.4%**	**-0.1%**	▼
People's Republic of China	Upper Middle	449.25	86.3%	64.2%	454.32	-5.1	-1.1%	▼	1.8%	1.7%	1.6%	1.6%	1.5%	-0.1%	▼
Japan	High Income	63.14	12.1%	9.0%	63.34	-0.2	-0.3%	▼	1.2%	1.3%	1.2%	1.3%	1.2%	-0.1%	▼
Republic of Korea	High Income	7.41	1.4%	1.1%	7.17	0.2	3.4%	▲	0.5%	0.4%	0.3%	0.4%	0.4%	0.0%	↔
Mongolia	Upper Middle	0.55	0.1%	0.1%	0.60	-0.1	-8.7%	▼	11.7%	10.0%	9.1%	7.5%	5.1%	-2.4%	▼
South Asia		**86.74**	**100.0%**	**12.4%**	**94.37**	**-7.6**	**-8.1%**	▼				**4.0%**	**3.5%**	**-0.5%**	▼
India	Lower Middle	56.31	64.9%	8.0%	69.41	-13.1	-18.9%	▼	7.9%	6.5%	4.8%	3.4%	2.5%	-0.9%	▼
Bangladesh	Lower Middle	20.27	23.4%	2.9%	15.80	4.5	28.3%	▲	7.7%	7.9%	8.2%	9.0%	20.2%	11.2%	▲
Sri Lanka	Lower Middle	4.58	5.3%	0.7%	4.35	0.2	5.3%	▲	4.9%	4.5%	12.0%	13.1%	12.9%	-0.2%	▼
Pakistan	Lower Middle	3.90	4.5%	0.6%	3.58	0.3	8.7%	▲	9.2%	7.9%	7.3%	7.6%	6.3%	-1.3%	▼
Nepal	Lower Middle	1.68	1.9%	0.2%	1.23	0.4	36.5%	▲	1.7%	1.2%	2.4%	3.8%	4.6%	0.9%	▲
Southeast Asia		**88.51**	**100.0%**	**12.6%**	**89.44**	**-0.9**	**-1.0%**	▼				**2.6%**	**2.6%**	**-0.0%**	▼
Singapore	High Income	12.56	14.2%	1.8%	16.33	-3.8	-23.0%	▼	2.6%	2.1%	1.8%	1.7%	1.3%	-0.4%	▼
Thailand	Upper Middle	14.45	16.3%	2.1%	14.35	0.1	0.7%	▲	3.1%	3.0%	2.7%	2.7%	2.7%	0.0%	▲
Indonesia	Upper Middle	10.08	11.4%	1.4%	10.05	0.0	0.3%	▲	3.1%	3.0%	2.4%	2.2%	2.1%	-0.1%	▼
Philippines	Lower Middle	8.63	9.7%	1.2%	8.08	0.5	6.7%	▲	3.6%	4.0%	3.2%	3.2%	3.3%	0.0%	▲
Viet Nam	Lower Middle	31.39	35.5%	4.5%	30.14	1.3	4.2%	▲	1.7%	1.5%	2.0%	4.6%	5.4%	0.8%	▲
Malaysia	Upper Middle	7.26	8.2%	1.0%	7.68	-0.4	-5.4%	▼	1.6%	1.7%	1.7%	1.7%	1.4%	-0.2%	▼
Cambodia	Lower Middle	4.13	4.7%	0.6%	2.82	1.3	46.5%	▲	2.1%	2.0%	3.1%	5.4%	7.0%	1.6%	▲
Central Asia		**4.60**	**100.0%**	**0.7%**	**4.10**	**0.5**	**12.3%**	▲				**2.8%**	**2.7%**	**-0.1%**	▼
Kazakhstan	Upper Middle	2.09	45.4%	0.3%	1.90	0.2	10.0%	▲	6.9%	3.3%	3.4%	2.9%	3.1%	0.2%	▲
Uzbekistan	Lower Middle	1.64	35.6%	0.2%	1.35	0.3	21.7%	▲	2.1%	5.1%	3.5%	3.5%	3.9%	0.4%	▲
Azerbaijan	Upper Middle	0.39	8.5%	0.1%	0.37	0.0	6.6%	▲	6.1%	4.6%	2.6%	1.9%	1.9%	0.0%	▲
Armenia	Upper Middle	0.48	10.5%	0.1%	0.49	-0.0	-0.8%	▼	4.5%	1.9%	2.8%	2.4%	1.2%	-1.2%	▼

bln = billion, NPL = nonperforming loan.

Notes:

[a] Original values are denominated in local currencies and converted to United States dollars ($), with exchange rates on relevant dates. The table only includes selected countries for which data was available and with the latest reported gross NPL stock of over $250 million as of 31 December 2024. Lower NPLs are shown in green and higher NPLs in dark orange on a graduated scale through the spectrum.

[b] For 2024 data, the cut-off dates are as follows:
- NPL volume and ratio: Japan (Q3), Sri Lanka (Q2), and Viet Nam (Q2)
- NPL volume only: Bangladesh (Q2)

For all other 2024 data, as well as 2023 data, the cut-off date is end of the year, unless otherwise specified.

Sources: Statistics published by central banks; CEIC Data; and International Monetary Fund Financial Soundness Indicators (accessed July 2025).

Figure 1: Nonperforming Loans Volume ($ billion) with Nonperforming Loans Ratio (%) by Region and Subregion

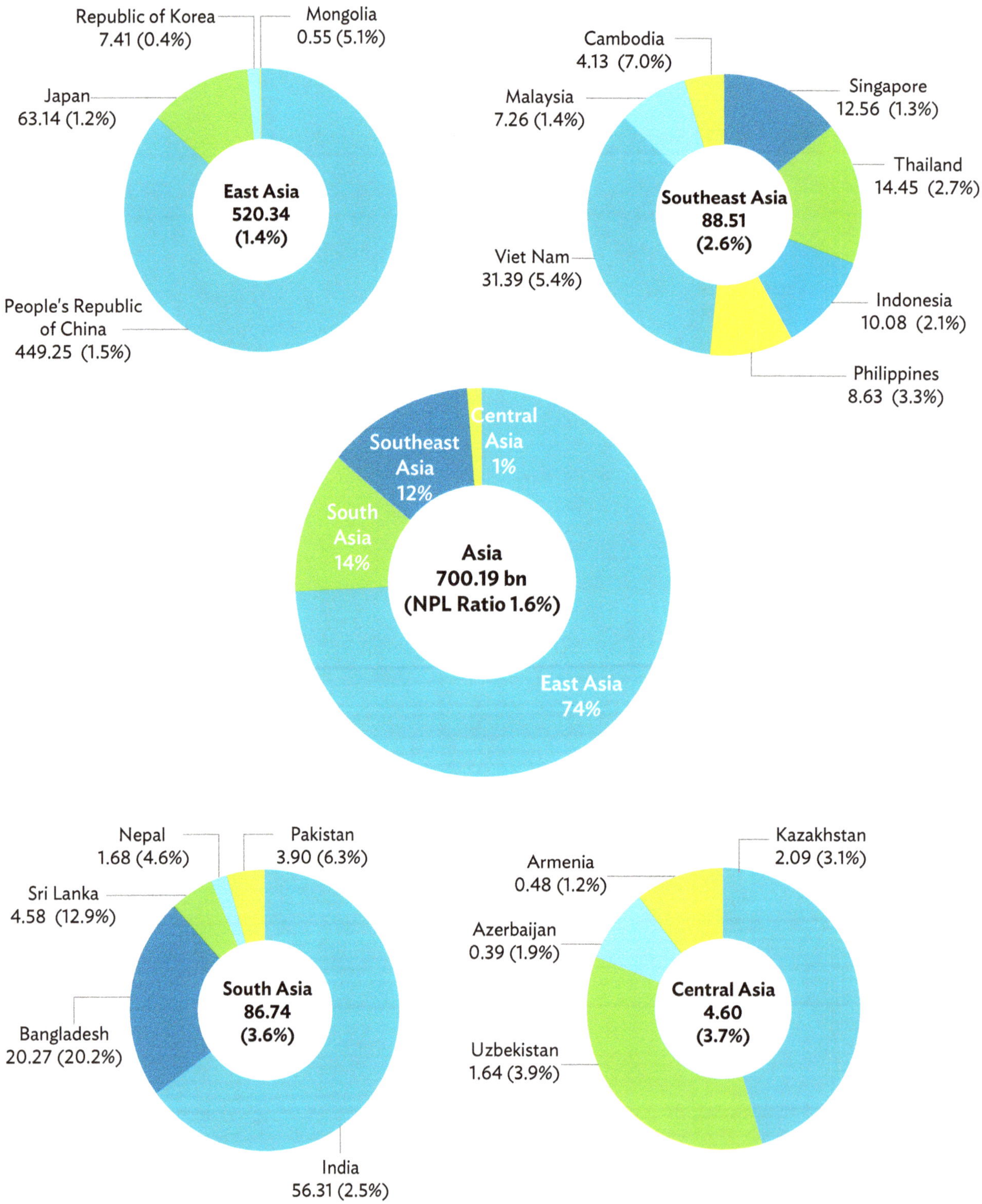

bn = billion, NPL = nonperforming loan.

Note: Due to the lack of publicly accessible NPL data, this report does not cover the Pacific region and focuses solely on Asia.

Sources: Statistics published by central banks; CEIC data; and International Monetary Fund Financial Soundness Indicators (accessed July 2025).

The PRC's NPL ratio declined from 1.6% in 2023 to only 1.5% in 2024, continuing a 5-year trend of gradual improvement. The low and decreasing NPL ratio reflects ongoing efforts to manage credit risk and resolve legacy bad debts, such as regulatory reforms implemented, strengthened risk management practices, and targeted interventions in vulnerable sectors such as real estate and local government financing. However, underlying credit stress may still be masked by delayed recognition or regulatory discretion, especially in sectors like real estate and local government financing, which require particular attention in the current macroeconomic environment.

According to recent ZSAMC analysis,[2] NPL performance has varied significantly across different categories of banks. Large state-owned and joint-stock banks have generally sustained lower NPL ratios, supported by more robust risk governance frameworks and diversified portfolios. In contrast, city commercial and privately owned banks have experienced modest increases in distressed assets, reflecting their greater exposure to regional economic pressures. Meanwhile, rural commercial banks have notably improved, largely due to restructuring initiatives and policy-driven clean-up efforts led by local governments. This divergence underscores the importance of institution-specific strategies and regulatory support in shaping NPL outcomes across the PRC's banking system.

Japan follows the PRC in share of NPLs, at 9.0% of total regional NPLs (12.1% of East Asia). Japan's NPL volume declined in 2024 by $0.2 billion (or 0.3%), reaching $63.14 billion. The NPL ratio remained stable at 1.2%, indicating that the decrease in NPLs was accompanied by strong growth in the overall loan book. This reflects a broader expansion in credit rather than a deterioration in asset quality, as the total volume of outstanding loans grew enough to offset the impact of existing bad loans.

The Republic of Korea's banking sector remained resilient in 2024. NPL volume rose slightly, to $7.41 billion, but the NPL ratio remained at a low 0.4%. Over the past 5 years, the country has consistently maintained one of the lowest NPL ratios in the region, supported by strong regulatory oversight and prudent lending practices. The slight increase in volume is likely cyclical and does not indicate broader stress.

Mongolia improved significantly, reducing its NPL ratio from 7.5% to 5.1%, continuing a multiyear downward trend.

South Asia

South Asia holds 12.4% of Asia's NPLs volumes, with total NPL volume of $86.74 billion, down 8.1% from $94.37 billion in 2023. Correspondingly, the NPL ratio declined, reaching 3.5% in 2024 from 4.0% in 2023.

India, the region's largest economy, showed decreasing trend in NPL volume of $56.31 billion and an NPL ratio of 2.5%.

Bangladesh stood out as a regional outlier, with NPLs rising sharply from $15.80 billion in 2023 to $20.27 billion in 2024, a rise of 28.3 percentage points year-on-year. Its NPL ratio also climbed to 20.2% (from 9.0% in 2023), one of the highest in Asia. This contrasts significantly to its NPL ratio of 7.7% in 2020 and likely indicates structural weaknesses in credit underwriting and NPL resolution.

Sri Lanka's NPL volume increased modestly to $4.58 billion, but its NPL ratio remains elevated at 12.9%, the highest in the sample of economies analyzed in Asia and up significantly from 4.5% in 2021. This suggests ongoing stress in the financial sector and structural issues requiring immediate attention.

2 Zhejiang Zheshang Asset Management Company. 2025. 2024 China NPL Market Report.

Pakistan's NPL volume also rose modestly, reaching $3.90 billion. Its NPL ratio stands at 6.3%, still elevated, though it has shown a modest downward trend over the past 5 years.

In Nepal, NPL volume rose sharply (36.5 percentage points) in 2024 and the NPL ratio also increased (reaching 4.6%).

Southeast Asia

Southeast Asia has 12.6% of Asia's total NPLs volumes. NPL volume declined 1.0%, from $89.44 billion in 2023 to $88.51 billion in 2024. The NPL ratio remained stable at 2.6% in 2024.

Of the best performers, Singapore led improvements, reducing its NPL volume from $16.33 billion in 2023 to $12.56 billion in 2024 and its NPL ratio to 1.3% from 1.7% in 2023, reflecting effective credit risk management and a strong macroeconomic environment.

In contrast, NPLs in Viet Nam continued to rise, increasing 4.2% to $31.39 billion in 2024 from $30.14 billion in 2023, with its NPL ratio rising to 5.4%, the second highest in Southeast Asia, and up sharply from 1.7% in 2020. Rapid credit expansion, particularly in real estate and consumer lending, and challenges in enforcement and resolution may have driven the increase. Strengthening supervisory capacity and early warning systems will be critical to managing these risks.

Malaysia's NPLs declined slightly, reaching a ratio of 1.4% in 2024 (from 1.7% in 2023), suggesting gradual improvement in asset quality. Cambodia continued to face rising NPLs, with its ratio reaching 7.0% in 2024 (from 5.4% in 2023), indicating growing financial stress. The Philippines also saw a minor increase in NPLs reaching 3.3% in 2024, while Indonesia and Thailand remained stable.

Central Asia

Central Asia reported the smallest share of Asia's NPLs, with only slightly above 0.7% of the total overall region's NPL volumes. Total NPL volumes reached about $4.60 billion in 2024, up 12.3% from $4.10 billion in 2023. Despite this, the average NPL ratio decreased 0.1% year-on-year, to reach 2.7% in 2024.

NPL volumes increased in Kazakhstan (10.0%) and Uzbekistan (21.7%) in 2024, although their ratios remained moderate at 3.1% and 3.9%, respectively. Armenia stood out with a 0.8% decrease in NPL volume, albeit from a low base, reaching $0.48 billion in 2024, while its NPL ratio declined to 1.2%. Azerbaijan's NPL ratio remained stable at 1.9%.

3 Asset Management Companies Nonperforming Loans Transaction Trends in the Region

Transaction activity is progressing—but most markets remain at early or moderate stages of development. Nonperforming loan (NPL) sales remain largely domestic—dominated by public asset management companies (AMCs)—with limited participation from institutional or foreign investors. This highlights the need to broaden buyer access.

The NPL transaction market in Asia evolved considerably through 2024 and into early 2025, supported by macroeconomic stabilization, targeted regulatory reforms, and gradually improving investor sentiment. While resolution frameworks are becoming more institutionalized in many jurisdictions, key market features—such as transaction volumes, pricing dynamics, and investor participation—remain diverse across the region.

This section reviews AMC-led transaction trends based on the 2025 IPAF survey sent to public AMCs across seven jurisdictions and in-depth interviews with AMCs in the PRC, the Republic of Korea, and Viet Nam. The figures present data on volumes, investor profiles, transaction structures, and sector distribution.

Overview of the 2025 IPAF Survey

- Target: 8 IPAF member countries
- Respondents: 10 institutions[3] from 7 countries[4]
- Period: 3–24 February 2025
- Method: Online survey via JotForm

Overview of the 2025 IPAF In-depth Interview

- Target: Three major contributing countries for this report (PRC, Republic of Korea, and Viet Nam)
- Respondent: four institutions[5] from three countries
- Date: 19 March 2025
- Method: Back-to-back calls via MS Teams (30 minutes each)

AMCs remain central to the NPL resolution architecture across Asia. In most jurisdictions, they act as direct acquirers of distressed assets, facilitators of secondary trades, pilot users of digital tools, and executors of financial stability mandates. However, the scope of these roles, autonomy of execution, and operational approaches vary considerably by country, as confirmed by survey responses and interviews.

3 Full list of the survey respondents: Agency for Regulation and Development of the Financial Market of the Republic of Kazakhstan, China Great Wall Asset Management Corporation, KAMCO, Mongolia Asset Management Corporation (MAMCO), PT Perusahaan Pengelola Aset, Sukhumvit Asset Management Co., Tianjin Binhai Zhengxin Asset Management Co., Ltd., VAMC, DATC, and ZSAMC.

4 The Agency for Regulation and Development of the Financial Market (Kazakhstan) is neither an AMC nor an IPAF member but provided a response on behalf of Fund of Problem Loans.

5 The four AMCs interviewed: KAMCO, VAMC, DATC, and ZSAMC. Interviews were conducted by ADB and Eric Cloutier, ADB consultant and partner at Forvis Mazars.

According to the IPAF survey, transaction volumes across the region are highly polarized. Around 20% of AMCs reported annual transaction activity exceeding $2 billion—primarily in the PRC and the Republic of Korea. In contrast, over 60% of respondents reported sales below $50 million or no activity at all. Institutional factors such as asset eligibility rules, investor access, and AMC governance models heavily influence transaction volumes at the national level.

Transaction execution in the region remains primarily from direct sales, with relatively limited NPL securitization. This is largely due to the structure of the transaction markets being centered around AMCs for primary transactions from banks.

The sector composition of AMC portfolios and transaction flows is concentrated strongly in secured corporate and commercial real estate exposures. According to the IPAF survey, these two categories are the most frequently held in AMCs' portfolios and transacted. Interviewees from DATC and ZSAMC attributed this to greater predictability in valuation and collateral recovery. By contrast, unsecured retail and SME loans remain underrepresented due to factors such as incomplete loan-level data, limited servicer capacity, and longer enforcement time lines.

The use of digital platforms remains nascent. The Republic of Korea's OnBid system, described in the KAMCO interview, is currently the most advanced in the region—offering transparent listings and regulated access for investors. Viet Nam's VAMC has launched a digital portal focused on asset visibility, although it remains limited in scope and coverage. The IPAF survey confirms that most other AMCs either do not use digital tools or rely on internal systems that are not accessible to market participants. The need for harmonized data templates and due diligence protocols emerged as a top theme across interviews.

Institutional mandates also continue to influence market behavior. KAMCO is explicitly prohibited from participating in public auctions to preserve space for private actors. And in Viet Nam, VAMC and DATC operate under separate supervisory frameworks (central bank and finance ministry, respectively), leading to different risk appetites and portfolio strategies. These differences were consistently raised during the interviews as core drivers of the operational models in place.

While these findings confirm that the region's AMC transaction landscape remains heterogeneous, the direction of travel is increasingly clear. Survey results and interview insights point to growing interest in structured transactions, wider use of digital tools, and regulatory adjustments to improve investor access. AMCs across Asia are progressively moving from policy-led warehousing toward more market-driven disposal and resolution models—albeit at different speeds and from varied starting points.

We develop these points further, looking closely at the IPAF survey results and detailed analysis of the PRC, the Republic of Korea, and Viet Nam.

Detailed International Public Asset Management Companies Forum Survey Results

According to the IPAF survey (Figure 2), activity in NPL markets was generally deemed moderate to low. The most common response was "Active" (45%), followed by "Low activity" (36%). Few respondents characterized their markets as "Very dynamic" with only 18% of respondents.

Figure 2: International Public Asset Management Companies Forum Question—Recent Nonperforming Loans Transaction Activity, Current/Past 12 Months
(% of respondents)

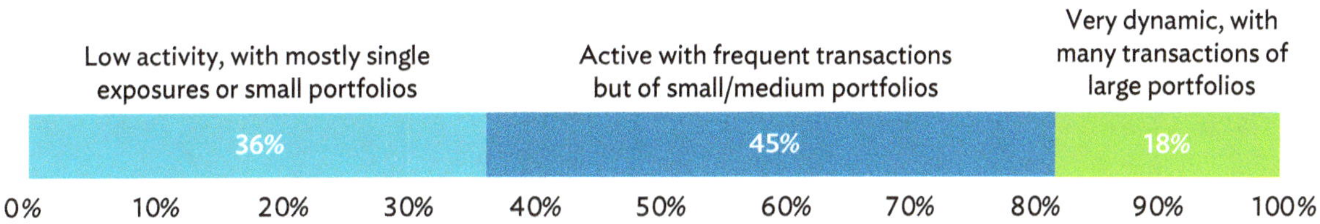

Source: Authors, based on a 2025 survey of IPAF members covering topics such as impediments to NPL resolution and sales, transactions activity, servicing capacity, and credit risks, and the NPL outlook.

This reflects conservatism in risk-taking by banks post-financial crisis and the significant regulatory obstacles to international transactions. This middle-ground assessment suggests that banks may be engaged in clean-up, but legal, pricing, or execution frictions still slow deal flow. Secondary market mechanisms—like trading platforms or public auctions—remain underdeveloped, resulting in bilateral, ad hoc, and often relationship-driven transactions. Moving to a more dynamic market will require scale, standardization, and greater buyer diversity.

By volume of transactions, the survey results (Figure 3) demonstrate that most AMC respondents estimated that over $2 billion in transactions had been realized in the last 12 months leading up to February 2024. This was followed by estimates of below $50 million, indicating the polarized field of NPL transactions among the economies in our survey group. Estimates were evenly spread in the following categories: $100 million–$250 million, $250 million–$500 million, $500 million–$1 billion, and other entries, each selected by 8% of respondents.

Figure 3: International Public Asset Management Companies Forum Question—Estimated Total Nonperforming Loans Transactions in Your Jurisdiction in the Last 12 Months
(% of respondents)

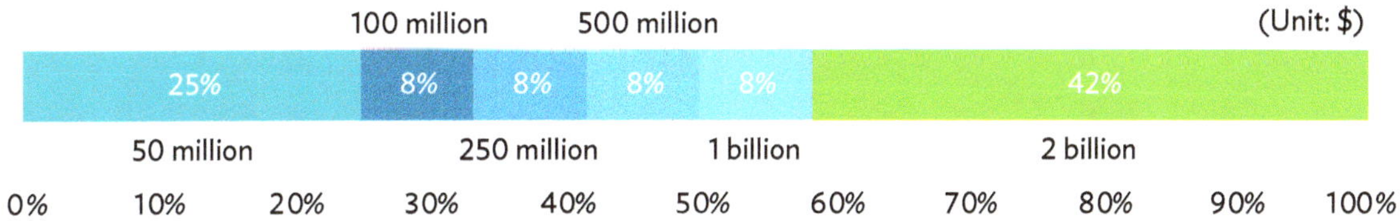

Source: Authors, based on a 2025 survey of IPAF members.

It is important to note that in the PRC, the two AMCs that we surveyed indicated an estimated level of NPL transactions between $1–$2 billion and over $2 billion. Compared to the total national NPL volume of $449.2 billion, this represents NPL transactions between 0.22% and 0.45% of total volume. Meanwhile, KAMCO indicated an estimated level of NPL transactions between $500 million and $1 billion. When compared to the total national NPL volume of $7.4 billion, this represents NPL transactions between 6.76% and 13.5% of total volume. The percentage of transactions relative to the total volume is even more variable in Viet Nam, given the differing responses by the surveyed AMCs. Indeed, the two AMCs we surveyed indicated an estimated level of NPL transactions below $50 million and over $2 billion. When compared to the total NPL volume of $31.4 billion in 2024, this would represent NPL transactions between 0.16% and 6.4% of total volume.

Overall, the polarization of transaction volumes—split between very low and very high ends—illustrates a fragmented regional picture. A small number of AMCs in large markets appear to drive overall volumes, while many others conduct limited sales, if any. This unevenness is not only a function of market size but also of preparedness: jurisdictions with aligned legal, regulatory, and institutional conditions tend to transact more. The limited activity in middle-volume ranges suggests that very few economies have reached a steady-state of transaction momentum. This dynamic is challenging for regional integration and points to a need for tailored reforms rather than a one-size-fits-all approach.

Similarly, the survey results depict a polarized landscape regarding NPL sales in 2024. While some systems exceeded $2 billion in transactions, a much larger group recorded sales below $50 million—or none at all (Figure 4). This underscores how NPL resolution in Asia remains concentrated among a few active jurisdictions. It also suggests that for many countries market-based resolution is still secondary to internal restructuring or regulatory forbearance. Without scaled transactions, it is difficult to establish benchmarks, attract a broader investor base, or generate liquidity. Raising transaction volumes will require a combination of stronger supervisory pressure, better data, and clearer rules on asset disposal.

Figure 4: International Public Asset Management Companies Forum Question—Volume of Nonperforming Loans Sales Performed by Your Asset Management Companies in 2024
(% of respondents)

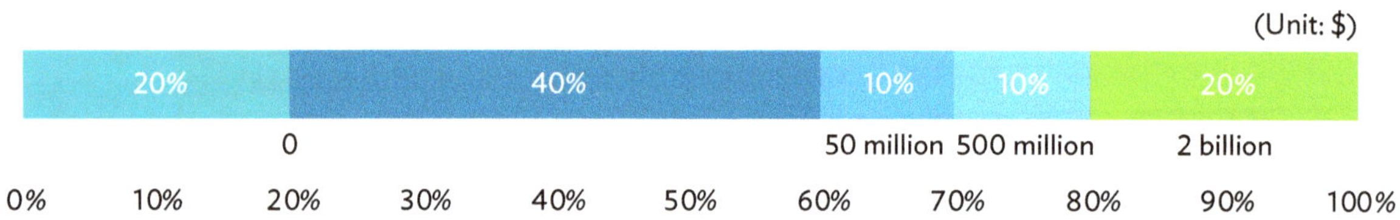

Source: Authors, based on a 2025 survey of IPAF members.

The survey results show that most Asian NPLs are acquired and disposed of within the domestic market, with the three highest responses being domestic investors or AMCs and public (state-owned) AMCs (Figure 5). By contrast, international investors were selected in 42% of responses as acquirers of NPLs sold by banks. This could be due to regulatory environments that make it challenging for international investors to participate. For example, in the PRC primary market, banks can only sell NPL portfolios to licensed national AMCs or regional AMCs. The lack of suitable platforms and technical capacity further limits the pool of potential purchasers.

Figure 5: International Public Asset Management Companies Forum Question—Who Banks Can Sell NPLs To (% of respondents per item)

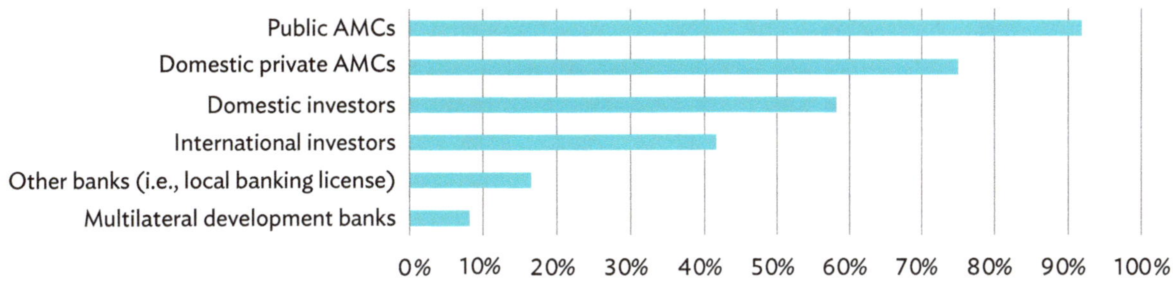

AMC = asset management company.
Source: Authors, based on a 2025 survey of IPAF members.

The dominance of domestic buyers highlights that many NPL markets remain closed or semi-closed environments, where transactions are confined to local institutions due to regulation or market preference. This internal orientation may ensure oversight and control, but it also reduces competitive tension and narrows the range of exit strategies for sellers. The limited involvement of foreign investors suggests barriers persist—ranging from legal eligibility restrictions to concerns around data transparency or enforcement time lines. Without expanding buyer access, especially in secondary markets, many systems risk remaining dependent on a small pool of repeat buyers, potentially affecting pricing and deal velocity.

The survey results show a fairly even spread regarding the three most active investors in each country: 92% "domestic private AMCs," 75% "public AMC," and 67% "domestic investors" (Figure 6). Notably, foreign investors are not included, highlighting potential regulatory obstacles or limited data availability from banks, leading to less interest from overseas.

Figure 6: International Public Asset Management Companies Forum Question—Types of Nonperforming Loans Buyers Most Active in Your Market (% of respondents per item)

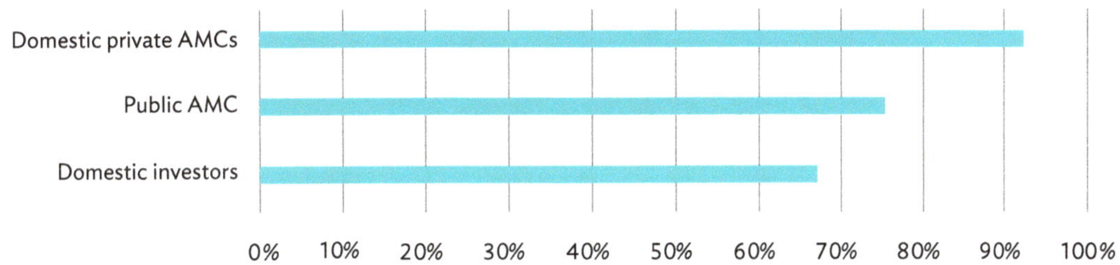

AMC = asset management company.
Source: Authors, based on a 2025 survey of IPAF members.

The buyer landscape remains concentrated, dominated by public and private domestic AMCs. This points to a market structure built around a small number of specialized players, often operating with privileged access to banks or regulatory support. The limited role of other investor types—notably foreign funds, institutional platforms, or capital market participants—suggests a relatively narrow base of demand. While this can ensure resolution capacity for standard portfolios, it also exposes markets to concentration risk: if a small group of local buyers slows or stops acquiring, activity could stall. Expanding the buyer base will be important to improve resilience and stimulate more diverse deal structuring.

Transaction execution in the region also remains primarily from direct sales. The IPAF survey shows that respondents identified at over 80% direct sales, either from banks to AMCs or between AMCs and investors, as being the main means of transaction. Only 17% of respondents identified NPL securitization used in the country. While bilateral formats provide flexibility and can accommodate jurisdiction-specific legal conditions, they reduce price discovery and limit benchmarking. Interviewees from KAMCO and VAMC also confirmed that bilateral negotiations remain the preferred model, often due to legacy relationships and institutional familiarity, rather than formal auction procedures.

In Figure 7, the preference for bilateral transactions reflects a desire for speed and legal simplicity, particularly in systems without established capital market infrastructure. The limited use of securitization confirms that structured exits are still rare, constrained by legal readiness and investor familiarity. As markets mature, however, direct sale mechanisms may face limitations—particularly in pricing efficiency and scalability. Introducing complementary models, such as structured notes or portfolio-based securitizations, could help increase asset turnover and unlock new investor segments. But that transition remains a work in progress.

Figure 7: International Public Asset Management Companies Forum Question—Most Frequent Nonperforming Loans Transactions in Your Country
(% of respondents)

Source: Authors, based on a 2025 survey of IPAF members.

According to the survey respondents, the most common sectors for NPL transactions were "corporate (secured)" and "commercial real estate," receiving 58% and 75% of responses, respectively (Figure 8). This indicates that credit risk attention should primarily be directed toward these sectors. Given the PRC's economic scale and recent weakness of the housing market, any crystallizing credit risks could significantly impact NPLs in the region.

Figure 8: International Public Asset Management Companies Forum Question—Most Common Sectors for Nonperforming Loans Transactions in Past 12 Months
(% of respondents)

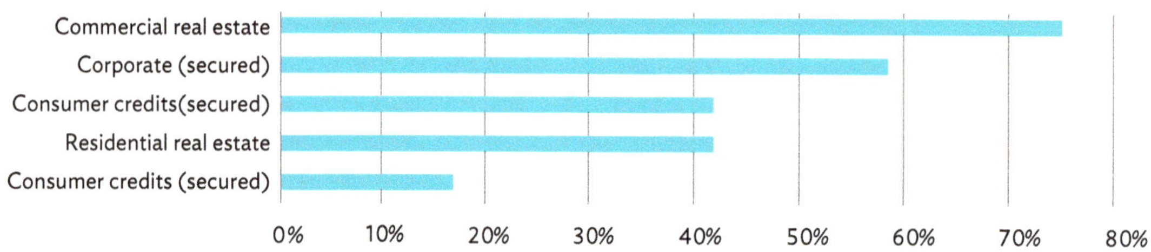

Source: Authors, based on a 2025 survey of IPAF members.

Following these, "residential real estate" and "consumer credits (unsecured)" were even at 42% of responses. The final category, "consumer credits (secured)," was selected in only 17% of responses. However, importantly in Viet Nam, such consumer debts do constitute a major component of NPLs, particularly impacting low-income households by impinging on their access to credit.

The concentration of NPL transactions in secured corporate and commercial real estate exposure loans reflects investor preference for tangible collateral and clearer recovery options. These sectors are seen as more "priceable" due to available valuation benchmarks and recovery history. In contrast, unsecured retail and SME exposures are less frequently transacted due to granularity, low ticket sizes, and recovery complexity. This sector skew highlights the need for better servicing capacity and portfolio aggregation techniques to expand liquidity across other asset classes. Until then, investor focus is likely to remain on large, secured, and relatively transparent exposures.

The survey responses in Figure 9, regarding the portfolio composition of AMCs' NPLs, largely mirror those in Figure 8, which detail the most common transaction sectors. "Corporate (secured)" and "commercial real estate" accounted for over half of responses cumulatively. AMC portfolios generally mirror transaction flows, with corporate and commercial real estate exposures dominating.

Figure 9: International Public Asset Management Companies Forum Question—Asset Management Companies Nonperforming Loans Portfolio Composition

(% of respondents per item)

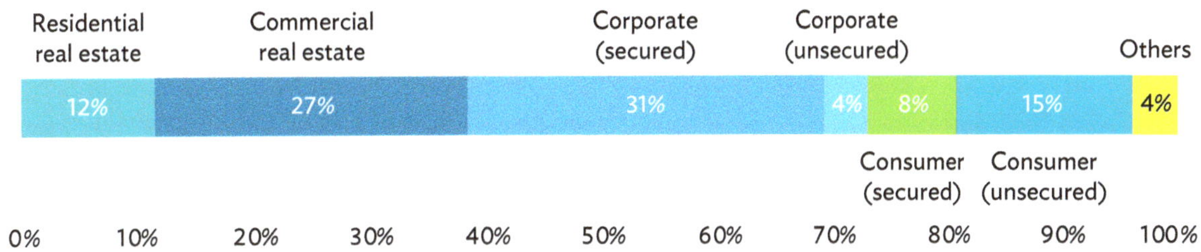

Source: Authors, based on a 2025 survey of IPAF members.

The overrepresentation of corporate loans in portfolios suggests these may be harder to exit due to restructuring complexity or limited secondary interest. In contrast, the lower share of real estate assets in AMC books implies they are easier to trade or resolve. The composition also shows that granular retail exposures remain a small portion of the AMC landscape, reflecting either limited supply from banks or weaker investor demand. Improving standardization and recovery channels for these smaller segments could help diversify resolution tools.

4 Impediments to Nonperforming Loans Transactions in the Region

Structural and operational frictions continue to limit market depth—but progress is visible.

While some countries have made significant progress in developing secondary nonperforming loan (NPL) markets, challenges and impediments persist across multiple jurisdictions, limiting the efficiency and attractiveness of distressed asset transactions. Key examples include information asymmetry between sellers and buyers, data issues, legal and regulatory limitations, inadequacy of judicial frameworks, and lack of deep and liquid secondary markets in some jurisdictions.

Our analysis of this section was conducted using a combination of methods: a questionnaire distributed to International Public Asset Management Companies Forum (IPAF) members across seven countries, interviews with selected AMCs in the People's Republic of China (PRC), the Republic of Korea, and Viet Nam, and references to empirical studies such as the report from 2021 by the Asian Development Bank (ADB) on "Nonperforming Loans in Asia and Europe—Causes, Impacts, and Resolution Strategies."

Summary of Regional Impediments

Based on the survey conducted with IPAF members, we can observe some recurring key impediments in the region to NPL transactions (Figure 10). Pricing gap between buyer and seller expectations (75%) and data issues, such as quality and availability (67%), are the most common impediments mentioned. Two related challenges received high responses; regulatory limitations (58%) and national judicial frameworks (42%), together nearly one-third of responses. Taxation regime (33%) was also identified as a key issue.

However, a broad range of impediments such as supply (33%) and demand-side (17%) impediments and inadequate market infrastructure (33%) also received substantial responses. This demonstrates the heterogeneity of the region in both the maturity of the national NPL transactions markets and the broad and varied legal, judicial, and structural environments between countries.

Further explanation of these impediments alongside their potential solutions are included in the country breakdown.

Figure 10: International Public Asset Management Companies Forum Question—Key Impediments to Nonperforming Loans Transactions Faced by Your Country
(% of respondents per item)

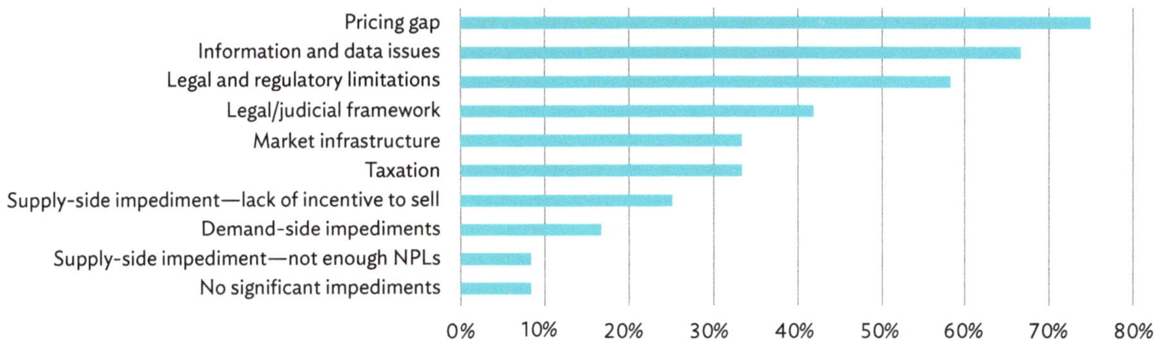

NPL = nonperforming loan.
Source: Authors, based on a 2025 survey of IPAF members.

Pricing Gap Between Seller and Buyer

First, persistent pricing gaps remain one of the most cited impediments to NPL transactions across Asian markets. These disparities are driven by a combination of internal bank valuation practices, regulatory capital considerations, and investor risk pricing. Survey results from IPAF members underscore this divide. Interviews with several AMCs and private investors also highlight that price discovery is often complicated by opaque data, limited due diligence windows, and inconsistent valuation methodologies.

The ADB (2021) report confirms these dynamics, noting that in many Asian jurisdictions, banks tend to delay NPL recognition or overestimate recovery values to avoid capital hits or reputational risks. This is particularly prevalent in systems where provisioning remains inadequate or where regulatory frameworks do not incentivize timely resolution or disposal of distressed assets. On the buy-side, investors often apply steep discounts to account for legal uncertainty, servicing complexity, and recovery time lines, especially for SME and retail portfolios.

These diverging expectations are compounded in less mature NPL markets, where transaction volumes remain low and benchmarks are scarce. While some AMCs have made progress in narrowing the gap—by providing pricing signals, facilitating secondary sales, and offering partial guarantees—most markets still lack the pricing transparency and consistency needed to scale transactions.

Information Asymmetry and Transparency Gaps

A key barrier to NPL transactions in Asia is the persistent information asymmetry between sellers—primarily banks—and potential investors (buyers). According to the survey of IPAF members, data issues, including poor quality and limited availability, is the third most cited impediment after pricing gaps and regulatory constraints. Interviews with AMCs across several jurisdictions confirmed that incomplete loan-level information, inconsistent valuation methods, and limited disclosure of recovery histories continue to erode buyer confidence and constrain deal flow.

In many markets, buyers lack access to standardized or centralized data, complicating due diligence and delaying pricing. AMCs often maintain internal datasets that are not shared externally, while sellers may provide incomplete or selectively curated information, especially for retail and SME loans. This undermines pricing accuracy and contributes directly to bid-ask spreads. Survey respondents also flagged concerns over the reliability of reported NPL figures, particularly in property lending and shadow banking, where true stress levels may be underrepresented.

Discrepancies in collateral valuation practices further compound the issue. Banks may rely on internal or outdated appraisals, while buyers apply more conservative or market-based assumptions. The resulting divergence in expected recovery values frequently delays transactions or prevents them altogether.

To address these issues, digital NPL platforms are being piloted in some jurisdictions to improve transparency and facilitate information exchange. However, survey responses and interview feedback suggest that adoption remains limited due to low platform coverage, lack of integration, and weak enforcement of disclosure standards.

This is the reason for the IPAF and ADB collaborative efforts to continue stimulating innovation in this area in Asia.

The May 2024 ADB report, How to Build Nonperforming Loan Trading Platforms in Asia and the Pacific, outlines a road map to strengthen transparency through harmonized data templates, consistent valuation standards, and improved information-sharing protocols. IPAF members have expressed strong support for these reforms, recognizing their importance in broadening investor participation and improving pricing efficiency across the region.

Legal and Regulatory Barriers

Overall, entrenched legal and procedural barriers continue to hinder the development of a robust and inclusive NPL ecosystem, limiting both domestic innovation and cross-border investment potential.

Variations in legal frameworks and the complexity of judicial processes across Asian economies remain among the most frequently cited impediments to the resolution and sale of NPLs in the region. According to the survey of IPAF members, regulatory limitations (16%) and national judicial frameworks (11%) together accounted for 27% of responses, making this—when combined—the most frequent impediment limiting NPL transactions in the countries surveyed. This underscores the systemic nature of legal and regulatory frictions shaping the region's investment landscape.

These challenges include restrictions on eligible buyers, fragmented insolvency regimes, protracted court procedures, and inconsistencies in enforcement mechanisms—particularly for cross-border transactions. Interview feedback from AMCs in multiple jurisdictions confirms that such barriers are not only procedural but often embedded in structural legal constraints and institutional mandates.

Among the most pressing legal challenges are the absence of dedicated courts for insolvency cases, a lack of early intervention mechanisms to prevent business failure, and the unavailability of tailored recovery options for small and medium-sized enterprises. Furthermore, investors are often unable to assume enforcement rights or hold collateral, which severely limits their ability to participate in asset recovery.

These legal and regulatory shortcomings have direct consequences for market development and platform implementation. One major limitation is the inability to resolve secured retail loans—particularly mortgages—which many banks are eager to offload due to their significant share in total NPL volumes. However, without the legal authority to enforce claims or take possession of collateral, investors are effectively sidelined from participating in these transactions. As a result, lenders and servicers often rely on cooperative or informal collection methods, which tend to yield lower recovery rates and contribute to a persistent mismatch in pricing expectations between sellers and potential buyers.[6]

6 IPAF Training 2025 – [Case Study] Cross-border NPL Investment in Viet Nam: Co-funding Partnership between IFC and Welcome Finance Group.

Weak enforcement of creditor rights can lead to prolonged legal battles over distressed assets and create uncertainty for buyers regarding the likelihood and timing of recoveries. This inconsistency may discourage investors from engaging in NPL transactions. Additionally, increased compliance requirements due to recent legal amendments can prolong the average resolution time line, making the process more cumbersome for investors. Strict regulations on foreign participation in distressed asset acquisitions also pose a significant barrier. These regulations deter international investors and, coupled with local courts prioritizing domestic financial stability over creditor claims, further reduce investment attractiveness.

Moreover, several markets continue to operate under non-harmonized legal frameworks, which can result in inconsistent interpretation of asset transfer rules and create barriers to the use of more advanced resolution tools such as securitization or structured sales. Even in countries piloting digital NPL trading platforms, the lack of clear legal backing for transactions has limited uptake and impact to date.

To foster the growth of scalable, transparent, and investable NPL markets across Asia, it is crucial to streamline and harmonize legal and regulatory regimes. Enhancing foreign investor access, strengthening enforcement rights and improving judicial time lines could significantly boost market activity and investor engagement.

Addressing these legal and regulatory constraints is essential to unlocking greater investor participation and enabling more efficient resolution of distressed assets across the region.

Unfavorable Taxation Regimes

Tax-related barriers remain a structural impediment to the development of efficient NPL markets across Asia. Interviews with IPAF members consistently point to outdated or overly complex tax codes as a material constraint on investor participation. In particular, uncertainty around the tax treatment of NPL transfers—especially regarding value-added tax, stamp duties, and capital gains—was identified by respondents as a recurring bottleneck.

Survey feedback further highlights inconsistencies in tax treatment across jurisdictions, which increase transaction costs and complicate cross-border deals. In several markets, the transfer of NPLs from banks to AMCs or investors continues to trigger full tax liabilities despite the distressed nature of the assets. Meanwhile, the absence of targeted exemptions or deferrals for NPL-related transactions stands in contrast to regimes in more mature markets. As a result, potential buyers often face effective tax burdens that erode recovery expectations and distort price formation.

The lack of harmonization, combined with opaque or discretionary enforcement, creates additional uncertainty and delays. Addressing these tax disincentives—through clearer guidelines and regionally aligned treatment—will be critical to unlock broader investor interest and scale up market activity.

International experience, as highlighted in the ADB (2021) report, underscores the importance of aligning tax policy with resolution objectives. In more developed NPL markets, tax frameworks are often structured to support timely disposal. This includes through measures such as full deductibility of loan-loss provisions and write-offs, and exemptions from value-added tax, stamp duties, or capital gains taxes on NPL transfers. These features help reduce transaction costs, improve price discovery, and encourage investor participation. In contrast, the absence of such provisions in many Asian jurisdictions continues to act as a drag on market development.

Nascent Secondary Markets for Nonperforming Loans

In addition to the top impediments identified by the IPAF participants to the survey, a fundamental challenge to the region is the lack of deep and liquid secondary markets for NPLs. Unlike areas where distressed asset trading platforms have become common, several economies rely on bilateral sales and government-backed AMCs to resolve NPLs.

In some regions, the majority of NPL transactions remain within state-controlled AMC systems. While such AMCs have evident and proven value, they can also limit external competition and the attraction of international investors. Moreover, private investors often face restrictions when acquiring distressed assets from banks, which further hampers market fluidity.

For instance, certain AMCs dominate the NPL market but struggle with slow asset disposal due to capital constraints and bureaucratic processes. This can be seen in various countries where AMCs are the primary entities handling NPLs but face significant operational challenges.

As mentioned earlier, to attract greater investor participation, some regions have launched digital NPL trading platforms. However, these platforms are still in their early stages, with low transaction volumes. Organizations such as ADB have advocated for the expansion of regional trading platforms, but widespread adoption remains a long-term goal.

Investor Sentiment and Risk Appetite

While global interest in distressed debt remains high, investor sentiment toward Asian NPL markets continues to be cautious and selective. Buyers remain sensitive to a combination of macroeconomic risks, regulatory complexity, and execution uncertainty—particularly in jurisdictions where transparency or legal predictability is still evolving.

Currency volatility remains a factor shaping investor pricing in several markets, particularly where external debt exposure is high, or policy uncertainty affects exchange rate stability. Even where recent movements have been moderate, the prospect of future depreciation is often factored into return expectations and recovery analysis.

Growth dynamics also vary across the region. While some economies are showing signs of stabilization, others face ongoing challenges in key sectors such as real estate and export manufacturing. Shifts in global demand, tighter financial conditions, and continued trade frictions—particularly with the United States—contribute to a more cautious outlook in several markets.

In this context, investors are increasingly focused on jurisdictions with clear legal frameworks, consistent enforcement, and functioning secondary platforms. Markets such as the Republic of Korea continue to attract relatively stronger interest due to institutional maturity and more transparent resolution pathways.

Appetite remains, especially among specialized funds, but broader and more sustained participation will depend on further progress in reducing market friction and ensuring predictable transaction conditions.

5 Credit Servicers in the Region

Servicing ecosystems are still developing; asset management companies (AMCs) often fill gaps where third-party capacity is limited.

This section draws on recent analysis from ADB (2024a), *How to Build Nonperforming Loan Trading Platforms in Asia and the Pacific* and the 2025 IPAF survey, among others, providing an overview of credit servicers' roles and emerging trends across Asia's NPL markets. Credit servicers—including AMCs, distressed asset funds, and third-party loan servicers—play a central role in the management, recovery, and resolution of NPLs. The structure and maturity of these entities vary significantly across jurisdictions, reflecting different stages of finance sector development, legal reform, and market openness.

Public AMCs continue to dominate resolution activity in many markets, particularly in economies where banking systems remain highly state-linked or restructuring policies are centrally driven. In contrast, more open systems have seen a gradual expansion of private sector involvement, particularly in higher-value segments or where distressed asset funds operate under special licensing regimes. However, survey data confirms that most respondents view their local servicer ecosystem as either "early stage" or "domestically limited," highlighting the operational fragmentation that continues to characterize large parts of the region.

While technological innovation and policy reforms are gradually reshaping the landscape, key challenges remain—most notably the scalability of servicer operations, recovery time lines in judicial settings, and the limited availability of portfolio-level transactions that enable efficient third-party management.

The evolution of Asia's NPL resolution ecosystem will depend not only on investor access and legislative clarity but also on the professionalization and market integration of its servicing infrastructure. Further progress will likely require coordinated reforms that go beyond AMC restructuring—addressing the entire value chain from enforcement mechanisms to asset monetization.

Deeper Dive Into the Results From the International Public Asset Management Companies Forum Survey

The survey results depict a varied profile in maturity and activity of the NPL transaction market (Figure 11). Only 8% of respondents stated that their country's market is mature, and 42% assessed their national market as being at the early stages of development. Meanwhile, 50% classified their national NPL market as inactive, mainly due to a lack of investors.

The results confirm a two-speed development across Asia. While some markets are mature, with repeat transactions and institutional frameworks, many remain at an early stage—still developing legal tools, investor networks, or transaction infrastructure. The absence of a significant share of "inactive" responses is a positive signal: most markets have at least begun transacting. However, the gap between mature and early-stage markets remains significant. Bridging this divide will be essential for creating a more cohesive regional market in the medium term.

Figure 11: International Public Asset Management Companies Forum Question—Maturity of Nonperforming Loans Transactions Market in Your Country
(% of respondents)

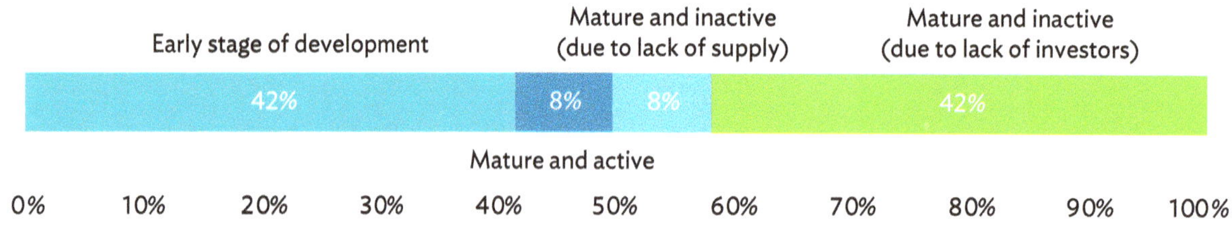

Source: Authors, based on a 2025 survey of IPAF members.

With half of the responses stating that the NPL servicers market in their country is either still local or at an early stage of development (Figure 12), the need for greater investment and expertise is apparent. Only 17% of respondents stated that the NPL servicers market in their country was "mature, with both local and international general and specialized NPL servicers."

Figure 12: International Public Asset Management Companies Forum Question—Maturity of Your Country's Nonperforming Loans Servicers
(% of respondents)

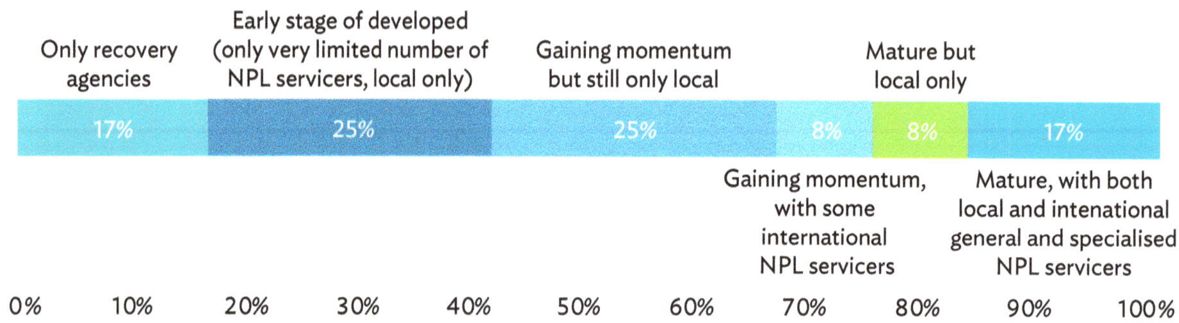

NPL = nonperforming loan.
Source: Authors, based on a 2025 survey of IPAF members.

Similarly, 17% of respondents indicated that their country's NPL servicers are comprised of recovery agencies only, suggesting an early stage of debt resolution infrastructure. This shows a high emphasis on debt recovery rather than resolution, with a more diversified range of NPL management solutions being restricted by complex regulations. The responses, where public AMCs and other domestic AMCs scored highest, support this view.

When combined, nearly two-thirds of responses can be identified as early stage of maturity, while 25% of respondents selected options that showed a more advanced stage of development of NPL servicers. The selection of "mature" or "gaining momentum" reflects a market with higher investor confidence and more sophisticated debt resolution strategies. Unlike markets largely occupied by recovery agencies, countries attracting international servicers likely have advanced methods for restructuring, refinancing, and resolving NPLs rather than focusing on collection. These markets benefit from regulatory frameworks that align with international standards and laws facilitating cross-border investments.

6 Credit Risks and Nonperforming Loan Forecasts

The world has changed in 2025, increasing credit risks globally. Attention is warranted. Effective credit risk management, early warning systems, and forward-looking provisioning are all crucial in today's more uncertain geopolitical and macroeconomic landscape. NPL growth is expected in select sectors—residential real estate, unsecured lending, and SMEs under pressure.

Credit risks across Asia remain uneven and closely tied to sector, macroeconomic, and regulatory factors. While most jurisdictions have avoided systemic deterioration in NPL ratios post-coronavirus disease (COVID-19), asset quality pressures are re-emerging—particularly in real estate, unsecured consumer lending, and SME exposures. These dynamics are shaped by the delayed effects of interest rate tightening, geopolitical uncertainty, and legacy vulnerabilities in market infrastructure.

This section draws on combined findings from the 2025 IPAF survey and interviews with national AMCs, as well as recent work by the KAMCO Research Institute, which employed deep learning to forecast NPL ratios and their key determinants across eight IPAF countries. Together, these inputs reveal a clear divergence: stronger systems like the Republic of Korea show controlled NPL growth under close regulatory supervision, while transitional markets—especially those with shallow secondary markets or lingering structural frictions—face more fragile credit dynamics.

Across the region, several cross-cutting themes have emerged:

- **Real estate and construction** remain the dominant contributors to projected NPL growth. Survey data and interviews confirm this trend in the PRC, Thailand, and Viet Nam. Developer strain, oversupply, and policy uncertainty continue to cloud asset recovery outlooks.
- **Unsecured consumer lending**, particularly in India, Indonesia, and parts of Southeast Asia, is flagged as a rising risk. Survey respondents identified this segment as the most likely to experience NPL growth in the near term, with inflation and wage stagnation cited as amplifiers.
- **Commercial and SME credit**, including vendor finance and short-term trade credit, is under pressure where post-pandemic fiscal support has tapered off. Respondents in the 2025 survey noted ongoing distress in export-dependent industries, including auto parts and light manufacturing.
- **According to the KAMCO model**, household debt, industrial production, and capital market conditions were among the top predictors of future NPL ratios. In the Republic of Korea, high household debt-to-GDP remains the dominant risk, while in Mongolia and Viet Nam, stock market volatility and corporate governance issues drive exposure variability.
- **Regionally**, macroprudential tightening is giving way to selective easing. Central banks in the Republic of Korea and Viet Nam cut policy rates in the first quarter of 2025 to support consumption, yet remain cautious due to credit quality concerns in specific borrower segments.

From a forecasting standpoint, the majority of survey respondents anticipate a moderate increase in NPL volumes through 2026–2027. However, expectations remain anchored in a base case of gradual deterioration rather than systemic dislocation. Approximately 80% of participants expect volumes to rise only slightly, reflecting a view that recovery trajectories will diverge more by sector and borrower profile than by country.

Finally, digital infrastructure, regulatory intervention, and market participation models are expected to influence the trajectory of NPL formation. Interviewees cited improvements in early warning systems and portfolio sales capacity as stabilizing factors, but warned that information asymmetries and legal execution gaps continue to weigh on investor confidence in several markets.

The following sections examine individual sector risks, national forecast paths, and the results of the 2025 KAMCO forecasting model.

Deeper Dive Into the Results from the International Public Asset Management Companies Forum Survey

According to the survey results, the main areas of concern regarding credit risk were identified as "residential real estate," "commercial real estate," and "retail," each receiving 21% of responses (Figure 13). This could be driven by factors such as slowing demand, regulatory pressures, higher interest rates, or high levels of debt in the real estate market. Additionally, there are concerns about the accuracy of collateral valuations and the industry's reliance on external financing and sensitivity to macroeconomic changes.

Figure 13: International Public Asset Management Companies Forum Question—Credit Risk Deterioration by Industry (Lending Area) in the Next 24 Months

(% of respondents per item)

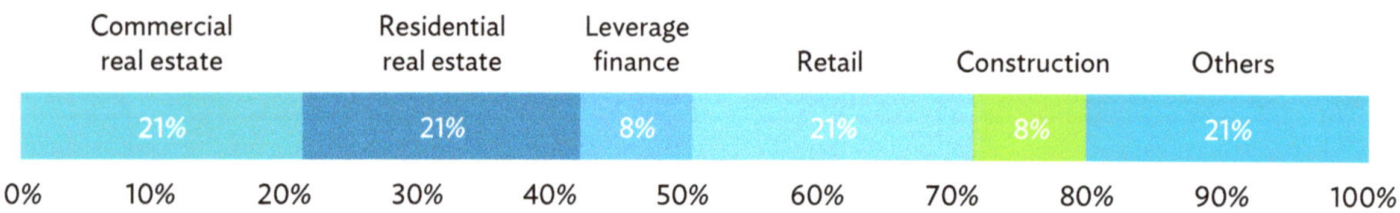

Source: Authors, based on a 2025 survey of IPAF members.

The next most common concerns were "construction" and "leverage finance," each with 8% of responses. The construction industry's ranking suggests worries about delayed projects, supply chain disruptions, rising costs, and cash flow issues for developers due to reduced confidence in the real estate market. These responses highlight concerns around industries vulnerable to economic cycles and interest rate volatility. If these credit deterioration risks materialize, stricter lending criteria may be introduced for these sectors to mitigate future risks

The two main growth areas for NPLs, according to our respondents, were "consumer credits (unsecured)" (28%) and "corporate (unsecured)" (17%) (Figure 14). The predicted rise in unsecured consumer loans indicates significant concerns regarding household financial distress, driven by factors such as rising inflation, interest rates, or stagnating wages. Unsecured financing, like credit cards and personal loans, is particularly high-risk due to the lack of collateral, meaning defaults directly impact lenders without asset recovery options.

Figure 14: International Public Asset Management Companies Forum Question—Expected Rise in Nonperforming Loans by Sector in Next 2 Years
(% of respondents per item)

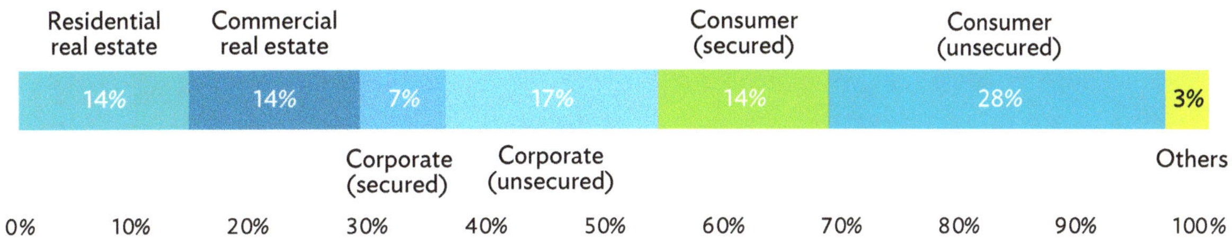

Source: Authors, based on a 2025 survey of IPAF members.

The expected rise in corporate unsecured NPLs reflects concerns around business solvency, especially for firms relying on debt financing without collateral. This could be due to global economic uncertainty, rising interest rates, or sector-specific stresses. Firms with highly leveraged balance sheets may face cash flow pressures, increasing the risk of default.

Overall, the focus on these two areas highlights concerns about economic resilience and debt sustainability where borrowers lack collateral.

The remaining responses were evenly split among "residential real estate," "commercial real estate," and "consumer credits (secured)," each selected by 14% of respondents. Both residential and commercial sectors face periodic downturns, possibly linked to tightening monetary policy, declining property values, or reduced demand. Similarly, some secured loans could see rising delinquencies if economic conditions worsen and borrowers struggle with repayment.

The areas of concern highlighted in Figures 14 and 15 are corroborated by the expectation of where NPL volumes will be in 2026 and 2027. Indeed, the 2026 estimates provided by respondents show a moderately adverse outlook with 70% of respondents stating that volumes would be slightly higher at this point. By contrast, only 20% instead stated that they would be the same, and 10% thought that they would be slightly lower.

Figure 15: International Public Asset Management Companies Forum Question—Expected Nonperforming Loans Volumes in 2026 Compared to Current Levels
(% of respondents)

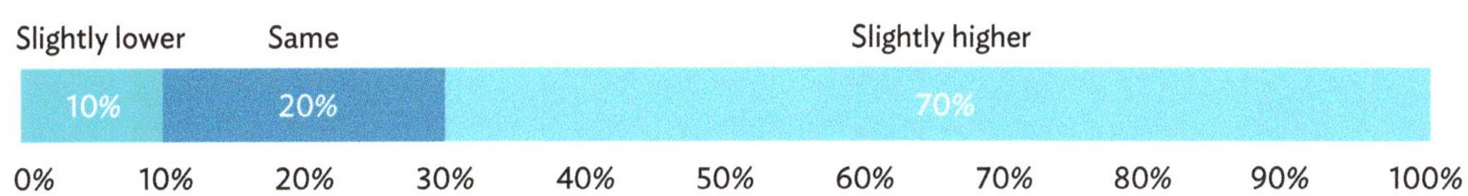

Source: Authors, based on a 2025 survey of IPAF members.

Similarly, respondents estimates of where NPL volumes will be in 2027 present a cautionary but not overly critical stance. Indeed, 80% of respondents determined that volumes would be slightly higher in 2 years' time, with 20% instead stating that they would be the same.

Korea Asset Management Corporation Research Institute Analysis on Forecasting Nonperforming Loan Ratio and Key Determinants in International Public Asset Management Companies Forum Countries

NPL risks are increasingly shaped by country-specific drivers—highlighting the value of data and predictive tools.

Figure 16 and Table 2 present selected results from the study titled "Forecasting NPL Ratio and Identifying Key Determinants in IPAF Countries Using Deep Learning," conducted in collaboration with KAMCO Research Institute as of March 2025.

Figure 16: Nonperforming Loan Ratio Projections for the Next 4 Quarters

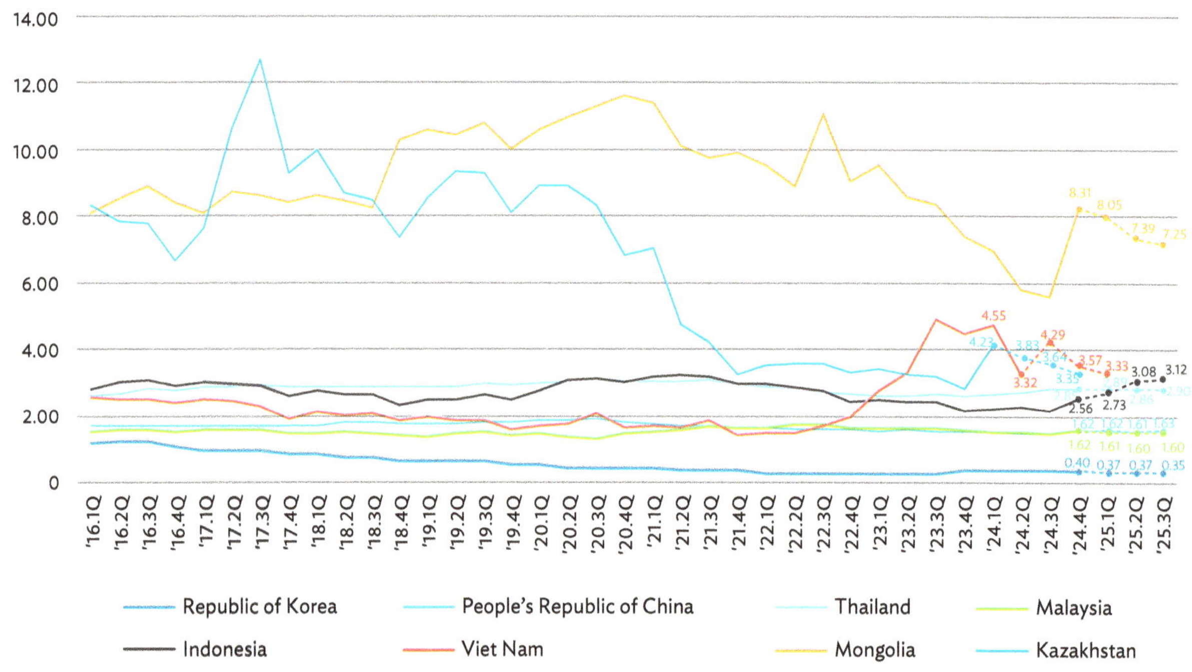

Source: KAMCO Research Institute.

The study found that NPL ratios of the People's Republic of China, the Republic of Korea, Indonesia, and Thailand were predicted with relatively high accuracy, while Kazakhstan, Mongolia and Viet Nam showed higher estimation error (mean absolute error, MAE). This discrepancy is mainly attributed to limited historical data and elevated volatility in past observations. Because deep learning models do not offer direct insight into variable importance, the study employed SHapley Additive exPlanations (SHAP) to interpret the results. The most influential macro-financial variables varied by country, and a summary of these key determinants is provided below. Further details on methodology and interpretation are available in Annex 5.

Table 2: Summary of Forecast Accuracy and Key Determinants of Nonperforming Loan Ratios
(%p, %)

Country	MAE	NPL Ratio Projections (next 4Q)					Key Determinant
		Point 1	Point 2	Point 3	Point 4	Summary	
People's Republic of China	0.02	1.62	1.62	1.61	1.63	Maintain	NPL Volume (past)
Republic of Korea	0.03	0.40	0.37	0.37	0.35	Slight decline	Household Mortgage
Thailand	0.03	2.85	2.89	2.86	2.90	Slight increase	Industrial Product Index
Malaysia	0.04	1.62	1.61	1.60	1.60	Remain high	Government Consumption
Indonesia	0.04	2.56	2.73	3.08	3.12	Sharp increase	Government Consumption
Viet Nam	0.15	3.14	3.90	3.00	3.31	Fluctuating	Market Capitalization
Mongolia	0.41	8.31	8.05	7.39	7.25	More volatile	NPL Ratio (past)
Kazakhstan	1.08	4.23	3.83	3.64	3.35	Less volatile	Government Debt

MAE = mean absolute error, NPL = nonperforming loan, Q = quarter.
Source: Authors.

Understanding Nonperforming Loan Forecasts and Determinants in Relation to International Public Asset Management Companies Forum Survey

The forecasted NPL trends and their key determinants can be further contextualized using responses from the 2025 IPAF Survey, as outlined below:

- **Republic of Korea:** Household mortgages were identified as the most influential factor in the model, highlighting concerns around secured lending—such as residential real estate, which accounted for 14% of reported exposures in the survey. This finding aligns with elevated consumer credit risk, reflected in the 28% of respondents citing unsecured consumer credit as a leading source of potential NPL growth.
- **Thailand:** The industrial production index emerged as the most significant determinant, suggesting a strong link between industrial output and corporate credit performance. This supports the survey result where 17% of respondents highlighted unsecured corporate credit as a key area of concern. As industrial activity slows, risks to corporate borrowers may rise, reinforcing expectations of elevated NPLs in this segment.
- **Malaysia:** Government spending was identified as the primary driver of future NPL dynamics. This is closely associated with infrastructure investment, given its scale and multiyear nature. A decline in public investment could indirectly affect credit conditions across both consumer and corporate segments, which were the top two sources of concern identified in the survey.
- **Indonesia:** The model forecasts an upward trend in the NPL ratio, which is consistent with expectations reported in the IPAF survey. Notably, 14% of respondents anticipated increases in NPLs related to secured credit—such as mortgages and auto loans—reflecting concerns about declining purchasing power and potential stress among middle-income borrowers.

- **Viet Nam:** Stock market capitalization was found to be the most influential factor, potentially reflecting the banking sector's exposure to market sentiment and foreign investor activity. This aligns with the 28% of survey respondents who identified unsecured corporate credit as a key risk area. Elevated foreign ownership in major banks may amplify sensitivity to market conditions, increasing the likelihood of NPL deterioration during periods of volatility.
- **Mongolia:** A general decline in NPL ratios has been observed since 2022, suggesting ongoing improvements in distressed asset management. This trend may imply that risks associated with secured sectors—such as residential and commercial real estate, each identified by 14% of respondents—could be less severe than initially anticipated.
- **Kazakhstan:** Government debt was identified as the dominant factor influencing NPL trends, indicating a stronger role of public sector intervention in managing financial distress. This policy-driven pattern contrasts with markets like Viet Nam, where credit risk appears more closely tied to capital market conditions.

7 Case Study of the People's Republic of China

The PRC has built the most extensive NPL infrastructure in the region, scaling up institutional depth and resolution tools.

Nonperforming Loan Transaction Trends

While the PRC's NPL framework is widely considered the most developed in Asia, ongoing transaction dynamics reflect a blend of institutional maturity and structural complexity. The following analysis outlines recent trends shaping volumes, investor activity, and resolution mechanisms in the country.

- **Market maturity and institutional depth**
  Formally established in the aftermath of the 1997 Asian financial crisis, the PRC's NPL market has developed into a multitiered structure. It includes 5 national AMCs, 59 licensed regional AMCs operating at the provincial level, 5 affiliated asset investment companies, and an expanding base of private investors. This diversity enables the market to absorb distress at scale and across asset classes.
- **Regulatory and supervisory framework**
  Oversight is jointly administered by the People's Bank of China, the Ministry of Finance, and the National Financial Regulatory Administration. National rules govern eligibility, risk transfers, and capital treatment, while provincial authorities have introduced complementary enforcement mechanisms. This layered governance ensures both consistency and local adaptation.
- **Transaction volumes and market activity**
  In 2024, over CNY214 billion in NPLs were transacted through formal channels. Despite a gradual decline in the national NPL ratio, the absolute stock remains elevated—estimated at CNY3.5 trillion. Regulatory scrutiny, particularly targeting regional banks, continues to drive supply, with real estate and construction sectors accounting for a growing share of volumes.
- **Primary and secondary market dynamics**
  In the PRC's primary NPL market, banks are restricted to selling distressed assets exclusively to licensed AMCs. National AMCs are permitted to operate across provincial boundaries, while regional AMCs are confined to their respective jurisdictions. Transactions typically take the form of direct portfolio sales, structured transfers, or securitized products.

  In contrast, the secondary market is more fluid, allowing interprovincial trading and limited foreign participation through indirect or joint-venture arrangements. Unlike the primary market, the secondary space is largely driven by end-buyers, including institutional investors and high-net-worth individuals. While large portfolios are typically acquired by major institutions, smaller bundles of distressed assets are often purchased by local investors. The absence of formal policy guidance and regulatory oversight in this segment has created a highly competitive, price-sensitive environment where deal terms are shaped more by market dynamics than by structured frameworks.

Despite growing activity, both cross-regional and cross-border trades remain operationally constrained by fragmented data systems, inconsistent legal interpretations, and regulatory bottlenecks. These frictions hinder the scalability and transparency of the market, particularly for foreign investors.

Foreign participation in the PRC's NPL market has shifted notably in recent years. Prior to the COVID-19 pandemic, international funds such as Oaktree, Goldman Sachs, Bain Capital, and CarVal were actively acquiring sizable portfolios.[7] However, the pandemic and its aftermath triggered a retreat, with many foreign investors scaling back or exiting altogether. Only a handful of firms with long-standing local presence have remained active.

- **Servicing and enforcement landscape**
  Resolution is supported by a wide but fragmented network of recovery firms and legal servicers. These actors operate at the provincial level, enabling local execution but reinforcing asymmetries in pricing, enforcement, and time-to-recovery. Coordination challenges remain where multi-jurisdictional portfolios are involved.

The PRC's NPL market continues to offer institutional depth, regulatory consistency, and high transaction volumes. Future development will likely be shaped by further expansion of the secondary market, improved data transparency, and continued innovation in digital and structured resolution tools. However, regional fragmentation and limits on international investor participation will continue to define the scope and pace of market evolution.

Analysis of Impediments

According to survey responses, market participants consider the PRC NPL market mature and active.

While the PRC's NPL market is one of the most developed in the region in terms of institutional architecture and transaction volumes, specific structural characteristics continue to shape investor participation, pricing, and transparency.

For those exploring opportunities, navigating the PRC's regulatory landscape can present some challenges to consider. Investments are subject to oversight by multiple government bodies at various stages, from initial approval to final registration. A deep understanding of procedural requirements—including licensing, filings, and compliance protocols—is essential for successful market entry and execution.

A number of structural impediments continue to influence the functioning of the NPL market—particularly around market access, investor eligibility, data transparency, and pricing dynamics.

- **Regulated market access:** In the primary market, NPLs may be sold only to licensed public AMCs—either national or regional. Regional AMCs are restricted to acquiring assets within their designated jurisdictions, which limits interprovincial transactions. This segmentation supports regulatory coordination but narrows the scope for wider market participation.
- **Investor eligibility and foreign access:** Foreign investors face procedural requirements, including the need to establish local partnerships. While these safeguards align with national financial stability objectives, they may limit external participation—particularly in the primary market.

7 Cross-Border NPL Investment in China: Market Overview and Foreign Investor Considerations – Kota Capital Advisors.

- **Selective supply from banks:** Larger banks often manage NPLs internally, while smaller institutions may hesitate to sell due to capital or provisioning constraints. This contributes to uneven deal flow and pricing variability across regions and counterparties.
- **Secondary market development:** The secondary market permits regional AMCs to transact beyond provincial boundaries and includes bilateral sales and auctions. While more flexible, this segment remains smaller in scale and more dependent on institutional relationships.
- **Information asymmetry and valuation divergence:** The lack of standardized loan-level data remains a barrier to scale. There is no unified market-wide standard for loan-level data. Investors rely on case-by-case due diligence, particularly for SME or retail portfolios. Differences in valuation approaches—internal assessments versus market-based models—further widen pricing expectations. AMCs also operate independently maintained systems, complicating portfolio comparability and slowing investor due diligence. Efforts to harmonize data templates are underway, but no binding national standard has yet been implemented.
- **Alignment of commercial and policy roles:** AMCs operate within a dual mandate that includes both market activity and support for broader financial system stability. In some transactions, considerations beyond immediate commercial return may influence asset resolution strategies.

The PRC's NPL market benefits from a mature institutional foundation and a well-established resolution framework. This is one of the deeper and most mature markets in the region. Continued progress on data standardization, transaction transparency, and mechanisms to broaden participation—particularly in the secondary market—could help unlock greater scale and investor diversity in the years ahead.

Credit Servicing

The PRC's credit servicing market is extensive but highly localized. The servicing sector comprises a broad mix of reinforcement companies, recovery specialists, and master servicers—many of whom operate within provincial jurisdictions. National coverage is limited, primarily due to the importance of local judicial networks, recovery infrastructure, and established relationships with courts and enforcement agencies. This localized model supports efficient collateral recovery but also results in a fragmented servicing environment. While regulatory support exists for further modernization, a unified servicing framework has yet to emerge, and standardized data sharing remains minimal, with each AMC maintaining independent systems.

Credit Risks and Nonperforming Loans Trends

Credit Risk Outlook

Credit risk pressures remain in many banks' performing books—particularly in the real estate sector and its upstream supply chain. Declining demand, falling home prices, and liquidity strain among developers have weakened borrower fundamentals. Related exposures in construction materials, industrial SMEs, and regional banks are also under increased stress. Provincial banks with high local real estate exposure are particularly sensitive. Monitoring of export-sensitive SME segments is also warranted, where weaker external demand and domestic currency pressures could further erode margins.

Nonperforming Loan Forecast

A moderate increase in NPL volumes is expected in 2026, with levels remaining elevated through 2027. According to the IPAF survey, and echoing the credit risks concerns, new NPL formation is expected to be highest in real estate, construction-linked SMEs, and certain manufacturing subsectors. While national AMCs have the capacity to absorb rising defaults, disparity in resolution outcomes might be observed between well-resourced coastal regions and inland provinces with less specialized resources.

8 Case Study of the Republic of Korea

The Republic of Korea's model combines institutional maturity with digital innovation—offering a regional benchmark for NPL resolution.

Nonperforming Loan Transaction Trends

The Republic of Korea's NPL market is institutionally mature and policy-aligned, with consistently low system-wide distress. While transaction volumes are modest, the market remains well-regulated, predictable, and operationally efficient.

- **Market maturity and investor ecosystem**
  The NPL market is anchored by a public–private model. KAMCO serves as the central public resolution vehicle, supported by private AMCs affiliated with financial institutions. This dual structure allows KAMCO to manage systemic exposures while enabling private actors to address sector-specific or niche asset classes. Transactions are typically structured through bilateral negotiations and are heavily influenced by asset type and regulatory preferences.
- **Transaction volumes and market depth**
  KAMCO reports annual transaction volumes between $500 million and $1 billion, representing only a fraction of the broader market. Total market size, including in-house resolution by banks and private investor acquisitions, is estimated at $55 billion. This shift reflects the increased role of internal credit management within financial institutions and low systemic NPL levels.
- **Foreign participation and market access**
  Foreign investors were highly active during the early 2000s but have largely exited the market due to reduced yields and increased regulatory complexity. Today, transactions are almost entirely domestically driven. The local investor base is characterized by high familiarity with Korean legal and servicing infrastructure, which remains a barrier to external entrants.
- **Primary and secondary market structures**
  KAMCO does not participate in competitive tenders to avoid displacing private actors. Most transactions are arranged through bilateral channels, with sector-specific targeting (e.g., real estate, construction). Secondary trades occur but are often bespoke and less visible, limiting overall liquidity and price discovery.
- **Digital platforms and resolution tools**
  The OnBid digital platform, operated by KAMCO, is one of the most advanced electronic transaction systems in the region. While its use for large portfolio sales is limited, it provides process transparency and helps standardize investor access. KAMCO is actively exploring further digitalization to support future scalability.

- **Policy alignment and compliance constraints**
  As a government-owned AMC, KAMCO is mandated to acquire and manage certain classes of distressed assets aligned with national financial stability goals. At the same time, evolving compliance requirements—such as those introduced under the Financial Consumer Protection Act—have increased the administrative burden on private AMCs and servicing agents.

The country's NPL transaction environment is defined by stability, institutional readiness, and policy coherence. While deal flow is selective and inward-looking, the system is well-positioned to respond to potential shifts in household or SME risk exposure. Future growth in market-based resolution may depend on balancing regulatory efficiency with continued innovation in deal execution and platform development.

Analysis of Impediments

While the Republic of Korea's NPL market is widely regarded as mature and well-supervised, a number of market-specific constraints continue to influence transaction flow, investor access, and the role of public sector institutions.

According to survey responses, respondents view the Korean market as active, with a clear legal framework and institutional track record. Key impediments identified include regulatory restrictions on market participation, limits on investor activity, and legal provisions governing the role of state-owned entities.

- **Defined legal roles and participation limits:** KAMCO, as a government-owned AMC, plays a central role in NPL resolution but is not permitted to participate in public bidding processes. This is intended to avoid distorting private market competition, but it also limits flexibility in structuring transactions.
- **Investor eligibility constraints:** Private financial institutions are permitted to acquire NPLs, but recent changes—particularly under the Financial Consumer Protection Act—have introduced new compliance obligations. These reforms aim to strengthen consumer safeguards but have also added complexity to private investor participation in recovery and resolution.
- **Selective transaction structures:** The market is characterized by bilateral, relationship-based sales rather than broad competitive auctions. This reflects both institutional familiarity and the preference for sector-specific buyers. While efficient in execution, this model may reduce transparency in pricing benchmarks.
- **Moderate transaction volumes and concentrated activity:** Although the market is active, deal sizes are relatively modest. KAMCO's typical annual volume ranges between $500 million and $1 billion. Survey responses indicate that a growing share of transactions now occurs outside KAMCO's remit, concentrated in private sales.
- **Stable legal and supervisory environment:** The country's regulatory framework provides clear oversight and requires banks to maintain low NPL ratios through internal write-offs and proactive resolution. This has supported financial system stability but results in limited supply of large-scale portfolios to the market.
- **Foreign investor interest and barriers:** International investor participation has declined over time. Whereas the market attracted major global investors in the aftermath of the 1997–1998 financial crisis, current levels of foreign involvement are more limited, in part due to the relatively low NPL ratio and a stable domestic investor base.

The Republic of Korea's NPL market benefits from a strong institutional foundation and consistent supervisory oversight. Significant progress has been made over the year to improve the frameworks to facilitate NPL resolution and develop a robust NPL transaction market, with the country being often referred to as a regional best practice. Continued efforts would be welcomed to further enhance depth and resilience over time, such as broadening investor access, standardizing transaction processes, and promoting competitive market mechanisms.

Credit Servicing

The Republic of Korea maintains one of Asia's most structured and predictable NPL servicing systems, anchored by KAMCO. KAMCO operates under a government mandate and does not participate in competitive bidding, instead absorbing assets that align with public objectives. Private-sector AMCs—linked to major financial institutions—complement this structure, specializing in collateral- and sector-specific recoveries. Although KAMCO engages in direct negotiations and leverages its OnBid platform for transparency, most high-value transactions remain offline. The servicing infrastructure is mature, digitally enabled, and closely supervised by the Financial Services Commission and the Financial Supervisory Service.

Credit Risks and Nonperforming Loan Trends

Credit Risk Outlook

The Republic of Korea's credit fundamentals remain solid, but there are emerging risk concentrations in a few areas. These include unsecured consumer lending, where household leverage has expanded rapidly, and SMEs in sectors such as logistics, retail, and energy, which face rising input costs and supply chain volatility. Commercial real estate exposures, particularly non-prime office and retail properties, are monitored due to shifting occupancy dynamics.

Nonperforming Loan Forecast

A slight increase in NPL volumes is expected through 2026, returning to stable levels by 2027 if macro conditions remain favorable. Survey responses point to expected deterioration in SMEs, unsecured consumer credit, and targeted segments of commercial property. Well advanced internal bank-led resolution and pre-default restructuring are expected to contain most cases before they reach default.

9 Case Study of Viet Nam

Viet Nam is making tangible progress—with institutional reform, digitalization, and market opening now underway.

Nonperforming Loan Transaction Trends

Viet Nam's NPL resolution infrastructure has evolved meaningfully in recent years, though transaction activity remains constrained by regulatory, institutional, and operational limitations. The market's development is shaped by its bifurcated structure and differing mandates between the two public AMCs.

- **Market maturity and institutional segmentation**
  Viet Nam's NPL framework is split between two state-owned AMCs. VAMC, under the State Bank of Viet Nam, manages NPLs originating from the banking system, with a focus on warehousing and resolution. DATC, under the Ministry of Finance, is tasked with debt acquisition linked to corporate restructuring, and the trading and resolution of debt through market-based mechanisms. Both VAMC and DATC characterize the market as still in an "early stage," citing limited investor depth and weak transaction repeatability.
- **Transaction volumes and asset flow**
  DATC reported 2024 acquisition volumes of $100 million–$250 million and disposals of $250 million–$500 million. VAMC's reported market activity was considerably smaller, with annual NPL sales below $50 million—This figure reflects only market value-based transactions and excludes those conducted via special bond structures. Transactions are mostly bilateral, asset specific, and small in scale. There is no centralized platform for price discovery or aggregated portfolio sales.
- **Market execution and structure**
  VAMC undertakes NPL resolution through public auctions of NPLs and collateral, while DATC negotiates NPL transfers individually, without auction mechanisms. Both AMCs engage in restructuring and recovery, including secondary re-sales to third parties, such as domestic institutional and individual investors. VAMC remains primarily focused on resolution and recovery within regulatory policy frameworks. This approach constrains portfolio-level trading and limits visibility for external investors.
- **Digital tools and platform development**
  Since 2021, VAMC has maintained an online portal for listing NPLs and sharing related data. While this platform has improved transparency and facilitated small-scale investor outreach, its usage remains narrow. The absence of real-time transaction functionality and broader portfolio access limits its role in scaling the secondary market.

- **Foreign investor participation and legal barriers**
  Regulatory requirements—such as the need to establish a local entity, restrictions on asset ownership, and project-level approvals—continue to inhibit foreign participation. According to DATC, past efforts by international investors to engage directly were abandoned due to administrative and legal complexity. Policy reform is being discussed but has yet to result in structural change.

Viet Nam's NPL transaction market is institutionally evolving but remains hampered by fragmented mandates, low investor diversity, and data constraints. Further development will depend on regulatory modernization, investor access liberalization, and the operational scaling of digital platforms. Without such reforms, transaction volumes are likely to remain episodic and limited in scale.

Analysis of Impediments

While the market has made progress in institutional development and digital infrastructure, a number of clearly defined impediments continue to shape transaction activity, particularly around legal access, data reliability, and pricing.

Two respondent institutions have differing mandates and asset scopes: DATC focuses on corporate restructuring and implementing government mandates, while VAMC targets personal loans and retail exposures. VAMC also operates a digital trading platform, which supports standardized processes in its segment of the market.

- **Legal and regulatory limitations:** Both AMCs reported constraints related to rules on eligible buyers and transaction structuring. For foreign investors, the requirement to establish a legal entity in Viet Nam remains a key barrier to participation and has led to the collapse of past cross-border initiatives. Regulatory clarity is improving, but restrictions continue to shape market access and execution strategies.
- **Taxation challenges:** DATC identified that tax-related impediments—particularly around the treatment of provisions, write-offs, and asset transfers—affect pricing, timing, and deal structuring.
- **Information and data quality:** Both AMCs cited issues with the availability, consistency, and completeness of loan-level information. DATC often conducts manual due diligence on a case-by-case basis, with banks providing varying levels of disclosure. While VAMC's digital platform improves accessibility, its current scope remains limited and does not fully resolve the data gap across the broader market. DATC supports the adoption of a national data model—potentially inspired by European frameworks—to improve transparency and enable more consistent pricing.
- **Pricing gaps:** DATC noted persistent differences between seller expectations and what buyers are willing to pay—particularly for corporate or real estate exposures where valuation is uncertain and recoveries depend on asset-specific conditions. The lack of standardized valuation practices exacerbates this issue.
- **Market infrastructure limitations:** VAMC highlighted the underdevelopment of supporting institutions, such as independent servicers or recovery specialists. This constrains resolution capacity and limits the market's ability to handle more complex or higher-volume transactions efficiently.

Viet Nam's NPL market continues to evolve, with signs of momentum in regulatory reform and digital infrastructure. Addressing impediments related to investor access, taxation, data transparency, and resolution capabilities will be essential to unlocking scalable investment opportunities and supporting more consistent transaction flows.

Credit Servicing

Viet Nam's servicing market is primarily supported by two public entities: the VAMC and the DATC. VAMC focuses on banking sector NPLs and operates a centralized online platform launched in 2021, which has helped narrow pricing gaps by improving visibility and investor outreach. On the other hand, DATC focuses on acquiring and resolving high-value debts composed of multiple collateral assets; consequently, its due diligence continues to rely on manual, asset-by-asset evaluations due to the absence of standardized loan data templates. Both institutions conduct debt restructuring and recovery services but note the lack of specialized third-party servicers and persistent legal barriers to foreign investor access.

Credit Risks and Nonperforming Loan Trends

Credit Risk Outlook

Rising pressure is observed in several segments of the banks' performing loan book. This includes personal lending, with unsecured consumer credit expanding faster than repayment capacity. Developers and corporates are also facing increased strain, particularly where project delays and financing constraints persist. SME exposures—especially in construction, regional infrastructure, and manufacturing—are also vulnerable due to interest rate sensitivity and weaker financial disclosure standards.

Nonperforming Loan Forecast

NPL volumes are expected to rise gradually through 2026 and into 2027. According to survey responses, the most likely sources of new NPL formation are residential real estate and unsecured retail lending. AMCs stressed that the pace of regulatory reform—particularly around enforcement and insolvency—will be critical in containing the impact and avoiding backlogs in resolution pipelines.

10 Conclusion

Asia's NPL markets are advancing—but scaling impact will depend on continued reform, innovation, and coordination.

Advancing the effectiveness of Asia's NPL markets will require a coordinated and forward-looking approach anchored in five strategic priorities.

1. **Evolve AMCs into full market enablers.** AMCs must continue their evolution from holders of distressed assets to active facilitators of market transactions, drawing on successful models from across the region, such as the PRC and the Republic of Korea, and supported by stronger governance, incentive alignment, deeper private sector engagement, and ecosystem building.
2. **Strengthen transparency through common standards.** Enhancing transparency through better harmonized data and legal frameworks will be essential to reduce transaction costs and improve price discovery. It is recommended to finalize the regional data templates and continue working on the alignments of the legal and regulatory models to reduce due diligence costs and narrow pricing gaps.
3. **Unlock broader investor participation.** Broader investor participation can be unlocked through more cohesive cross-border engagement strategies and the development of trusted. This can be supported through regional marketing coordination, further local engagement, and the development of investor-oriented platforms anchored by trusted institutions.
4. **Scale digital infrastructure with market integration in mind.** At the same time, digital infrastructure must be scaled with regional integration in mind. From national portals to regional data hubs, next-generation platforms will need to prioritize interactivity, benchmarking, and user-centric design.
5. **Tailor resolution tools to sector-specific risks.** Early warning systems, transaction frameworks, and tailored resolution tools will be needed to address emerging risks in key sectors such as real estate, SMEs, and unsecured lending, while remaining consistent with broader macroprudential and financial stability objectives.

These efforts all must continue to be underpinned by deep regional financial cooperation. By working together, economies in the region can better harness the benefits of integration while safeguarding against systemic vulnerabilities.

A more resilient domestic investor base, combined with broader attractiveness to international investors, will also be essential to support long-term soundness of the region NPLs' secondary market.

Together, these measures form a comprehensive road map for building a more integrated, transparent, and resilient financial ecosystem across Asia.

Annex 1: International Public Asset Management Companies Forum

The International Public Asset Management Companies Forum (IPAF)[1] serves as a key platform for public asset management companies (AMCs) and deposit insurance corporations across Asia and beyond to coordinate on strategies for resolving nonperforming loans (NPLs), strengthening market practices, and enhancing cross-border cooperation.

Initiated with support from the Asian Development Bank (ADB), IPAF has grown into a regional institution for dialogue, technical assistance, and peer learning among national AMCs and financial stability actors.

Activities

IPAF conducts various activities to achieve its mission. These include annual summit meetings and conferences, which provide a venue for addressing global economic and financial policies and issues. These summits also serve as a platform for members to define strategies and develop concrete action plans. Additionally, IPAF organizes training seminars and workshops aimed at sharing knowledge and experience, enhancing distressed asset management capacities among IPAF members, ADB developing member country governmental officials, and other invited participants.

In September 2024, Zhejiang Zheshang Asset Management Company (ZSAMC) took on the IPAF chairmanship along with Zhejiang International Business Group Co., Ltd. and successfully hosted the 8th IPAF Summit and International Conference in Hangzhou, People's Republic of China, under the theme *"New Era, New Paradigm, New Mission: Synergy Towards Asia's Financial Safety and Stability."* Following this, the 9th IPAF Training Seminar was also held, providing in-depth discussions, case studies, and technical training on NPL resolutions.

Resource persons and participants at the 8th IPAF International Conference on 12 September 2024 and at the 9th IPAF Training Seminar on 13-14 May 2025, both held in Hangzhou, PRC.

[1] Home - International Public AMC Forum; IPAF brochure.

In August 2025, the Mongolia Asset Management Company (MAMCO) will assume the IPAF chairmanship, together with the Deposit Insurance Corporation of Mongolia and the Bank of Mongolia, to host to 9th IPAF Summit and Conference.

Knowledge Sharing

The organization produces knowledge products and services, such as major research papers and case studies on the successes and failures of public AMCs in the region. It also conducts policy dialogue with policymakers on financial vulnerability issues, particularly distressed assets and nonperforming loans, and practices of AMCs in the region. An e-Knowledge platform is available to members, providing online access to relevant information, research papers, reference materials, training schedules, and networking data.

Developing Investor-Friendly Nonperforming Loan Markets in Asia

The IPAF has become a cornerstone in Asia's efforts to build resilient, transparent, and investor-friendly NPL markets. Its focus on digitalization, capacity building, and policy harmonization is enabling national AMCs to adopt best-in-class tools while tailoring solutions to local legal and financial environments. As NPL volumes evolve amid economic uncertainty, the IPAF's influence is expected to expand in shaping how Asia manages distressed assets in the coming decade.

Membership

The IPAF comprises two types of membership: general members and associate members. General members are public AMCs and institutions, while associate members include other relevant institutions. ADB supports the organization through a regional technical assistance project, and the IPAF Secretariat is based at ADB headquarters in Manila, providing administrative support. It has 18 members from 8 countries.

Year	Country	Name of Institution	Website
		General Members	
2013	KOR	Korea Asset Management Corporation (KAMCO)	https://www.kamco.or.kr
	THA	Sukhumvit Asset Management Co., Ltd. (SAM)	https://sam.or.th
	PRC	China Cinda Asset Management Co., Ltd. (CINDA)	https://www.cinda.com.cn
	PRC	China Great Wall Asset Management Corporation, Ltd. (GWAMCC)	https://www.gwamcc.com
	PRC	China CITIC Financial Asset Management Co., Ltd. (Former China Huarong Asset Management Co., CHAMC)	https://www.chamc.com.cn
	VIE	Viet Nam's Debt and Asset Trading Corporation (DATC)	http://datc.com.vn/portal/Home/default.aspx
2014	PRC	China Orient Asset Management Corporation (COAMC)	https://www.coamc.com.cn
	PRC	Zhejiang Zheshang Asset Management Corporation Co., Ltd. (ZSAMC)	https://www.stocke.com.cn
2017	VIE	Viet Nam Asset Management Corporation (VAMC)	https://sbvamc.vn/
2019	INO	PT Perusahaan Pengelola Aset (Persero) (PPA)	https://www.ptppa.com
2022	MON	Mongolia Asset Management Corporation (MAMCO)	http://www.mamco.mn

continued on next page

Table continued

Year	Country	Name of Institution	Website
Associate Members			
2013	KAZ	Joint Stock Company "Fund of Problem Loans" (FPL)	https://fpl.kz
2014	KOR	Korea Deposit Insurance Corporation (KDIC)	https://www.kdic.or.kr
2015	THA	Deposit Protection Agency (DPA)	https://www.dpa.or.th
2016	MAL	Perbadanan Insurans Deposit Malaysia (PIDM)	https://www.pidm.gov.my
2023	MON	Deposit Insurance Corporation of Mongolia (DICoM)	https://dicom.mn
2024	KAZ	Recovered Asset Management Company (RAMCO)	https://kuva.kz/en/
2024	PRC	Tianjin Binhai Zhengxin Asset Management Co., Ltd.	https://www.zhengxinamc.com

PRC = People's Republic of China, INO = Indonesia, KAZ = Kazakhstan, KOR = Republic of Korea, MAL = Malaysia, MON = Mongolia, THA = Thailand, VIE = Viet Nam.

Source: Authors.

Annex 2: Nonperforming Loans in Asia and Europe—Causes, Impacts, and Resolution Strategies

The December 2021 Asian Development Bank (ADB) report, Nonperforming Loans in Asia and Europe: Causes, Impacts, and Resolution Strategies, remains a relevant reference for understanding the structural and policy challenges affecting NPL resolution in Asia. The report provides a detailed assessment of the legacy barriers that continue to shape the region's nonperforming loan (NPL) markets. Many of its findings remain applicable in 2025, as several jurisdictions still face delays in legal reform, weak enforcement regimes, and limited investor access.

The report underscored the importance of Asset Management Companies (AMCs) in supporting national efforts to resolve NPLs. It highlighted models implemented in the Republic of Korea (KAMCO), Malaysia (Danaharta), and Viet Nam (VAMC). These institutions have contributed to avoiding fire sales, centralizing restructuring capabilities, and creating conditions for more active secondary markets. In 2025, these lessons remain relevant for markets still faced with structural constraints that limit the entry of private capital and international investors.

The report also pointed to several persistent impediments to NPL sales—many of which are still present. These include legal restrictions on asset transfers below book value, underdeveloped insolvency frameworks, and a reluctance by banks to accept market-based pricing. The combination of these factors continues to limit transaction volumes and widen bid–ask spreads, particularly in less mature markets.

The report highlighted the role of data transparency and digital infrastructure in supporting investor confidence. It recommended the development of centralized loan data repositories, electronic trading platforms, and standardized documentation—all aimed at reducing information asymmetry and increasing price discovery. While some of these recommendations have been adopted in the People's Republic of China, India, and the Republic of Korea, they remain largely unaddressed in other parts of the region. In 2025, these proposals are even more relevant given the increase in international capital targeting Asian distressed debt markets.

On securitization, the report made the case for developing frameworks to allow NPL portfolios to be structured into marketable instruments. Although progress has been made in markets such as the People's Republic of China and the Republic of Korea, most Association of Southeast Asian Nations members have yet to build the legal and regulatory architecture needed to support asset-backed NPL transactions.

Finally, the report called for greater regional coordination in regulatory and legal frameworks, noting that inconsistent definitions and fragmented enforcement standards continue to undermine cross-border investor interest. These findings helped frame the rationale for later initiatives such as the International Public Asset Management Companies Forum. In 2025, the call for convergence remains highly relevant, particularly as international investors seek more consistent rules and market infrastructure across jurisdictions.

ADB's 2021 report remains a reference point, as many of its findings are still directly relevant to current challenges in scaling efficient, transparent, and investable NPL markets across the region.

Annex 3: Practical Insights from the ADB 2024 Report on Nonperforming Loan Trading Platforms in Asia

The May 2024 ADB report, How to Build Nonperforming Loan Trading Platforms in Asia and the Pacific, provides a practical and policy-relevant framework for strengthening NPL resolution infrastructure through the development of electronic trading platforms. Its findings are highly complementary to the broader nonperforming loan (NPL) market analysis, offering actionable recommendations for jurisdictions seeking to expand secondary markets and attract institutional investors.

The NPL watch leverages the barriers to efficient NPL transactions highlighted in ADB (2024a). In particular, banks often fail to provide investors with sufficient, consistent, and granular information on loan performance, collateral characteristics, and enforcement status. This lack of standardized loan-level data creates significant uncertainty in asset valuation, which ultimately impacts the pricing of transactions—leading to persistently high bid–ask spreads and weak price discovery. These inefficiencies are especially acute in markets where legal frameworks are still evolving and digital infrastructure remains limited.

To address these issues, the report advocates for the development of purpose-built electronic NPL trading platforms, underpinned by common data standards, transparency in bidding processes, and investor protections. The Republic of Korea's OnBid platform, managed by KAMCO, is cited as a benchmark—illustrating how structured digital platforms can facilitate market access, reduce transaction costs, and support institutional investor participation. Key success factors include public sector sponsorship, legal certainty, and operational independence.

The report proposes the introduction of an Asia-specific data template, adapted from the European Banking Authority's framework but tailored to local specificities. This includes fields covering land lease expirations, enforcement stage, and asset recovery history—details that are often material to international investors but inconsistently disclosed across the region.

It also stresses the importance of regulatory alignment in enabling platform adoption at scale. Recommendations include the establishment of accreditation regimes for platform operators, mandatory use of harmonized templates, and legal recognition of electronic transactions.

Finally, the report calls for greater regional coordination, particularly in the context of cross-border NPL transactions. Harmonizing platform architecture, documentation, and data models is viewed as essential to increasing investor confidence and cross-border liquidity. These recommendations are aligned with the ongoing work of the International Public Asset Management Companies Forum (IPAF).

The report offers a clear and pragmatic blueprint for building the digital infrastructure required to support more transparent and investable NPL markets across Asia. As regional authorities and market participants move to strengthen resolution frameworks, platform-based models are expected to play a central role in scaling investor access and accelerating balance sheet repair.

Annex 4: The European Union Best-Execution Guidelines—Lessons Learned Relevant for Asian Nonperforming Loans Markets

The European Commission's 2022 Guidelines on best-execution processes for NPL transactions (2022/C 405/01) were developed to support the implementation of the EU Action Plan aimed at preventing a future build-up of nonperforming loans (NPLs) in the European Union (EU).

The aim was to facilitate more efficient and transparent transactions on secondary markets, while expanding the investor base and promoting greater integration of fragmented national markets. For Asia, the document provides a valuable set of policy-relevant insights and technical reference points, particularly as the region continues efforts to attract international capital and promote a more harmonized approach to NPL resolution.

The guidelines are built around a structured and phased transaction model, anchored by a two-stage sale process—nonbinding and binding offers—supported by standardized data disclosure, clear time lines, and virtual data rooms (VDRs). This approach is designed to enhance execution discipline and mitigate operational and reputational risks. Such a framework offers concrete lessons for Asian jurisdictions seeking to professionalize NPL transactions and build credibility among international investors.

A key emphasis is placed on data quality and consistency. The framework recommends the preparation of standardized loan data tapes, using templates aligned with the European Banking Authority NPL data standards, and supported by vendor due diligence and clear documentation protocols. These measures are intended to reduce valuation uncertainty, narrow bid–ask spreads, and enable better pricing. This focus is particularly relevant for countries in Asia where inconsistent data formats, incomplete collateral information, and fragmented disclosure still remain barriers to scaling NPL transactions.

The guidelines also provide a detailed road map for sale preparation, including defining the portfolio perimeter, ensuring internal governance readiness, and sequencing transaction steps. These recommendations are especially relevant for smaller banks and first-time sellers—segments common in several Asian markets—where internal capabilities for structured transactions are still developing.

Digital infrastructure is presented as a core enabler of best execution. The use of VDRs and online bidding platforms is shown to improve investor participation, streamline due diligence, and maintain process integrity. The Republic of Korea's OnBid system and India's IBBI auction portals already mirror parts of this approach, but broader adoption across the region remains uneven. The EU experience highlights the value of combining legal enforceability with digital tools to enhance market transparency.

Another central theme is the need for regulatory clarity. The guidelines outline key considerations around loan transferability, borrower notification, tax treatment, and servicing rights—factors that still present friction in many parts of Asia. The EU's Credit Servicers and Credit Purchasers Directive is cited as an example of how regulatory alignment can support cross-border participation and build investor confidence.

Finally, the framework promotes competitive tension and transparency as critical to price discovery. Open investor outreach, standardized documentation, and independent advisory support are encouraged throughout the process. These principles are increasingly relevant in Asia, where deal flow is growing but investor access often remains concentrated among domestic asset management companies or informal bilateral channels.

The guidelines offer a practical reference for Asia as the region seeks to expand its international investor base and develop a more integrated and investable NPL market infrastructure. While regulatory and market conditions vary, the underlying principles—data standardization, process discipline, legal clarity, and digital enablement—are highly transferable and essential to scaling investor participation across borders.

Annex 5: Forecasting Nonperforming Loan Ratio and Identifying Key Determinants in International Public Asset Management Companies Forum Countries Using Deep Learning

Preliminary Findings in Collaboration with KAMCO Research Institute
(As of March 2025)

This study explores the use of deep learning models to forecast nonperforming loan (NPL) ratios and identify their key determinants across eight International Public Asset Management Companies Forum member countries. Leveraging country-specific macroeconomic and financial variables, a two-layer long short-term memory (LSTM) model was selected based on performance. SHAP analysis was employed to ensure interpretability by identifying top contributing factors for each country. The findings suggest that while model performance is robust in countries with high-quality data, forecasts in countries with shorter or more volatile time series may lead to less stable forecasts. Country-level insights highlight varied drivers of NPL ratios, such as household debt, industrial production, government spending, and stock market capitalization. These insights provide a foundation for enhancing financial surveillance and informing policy decisions aimed at strengthening economic resilience.

1. Introduction

- **Objective:** This study aims to estimate the NPL ratio and identify its key determinants using deep learning algorithms. Deep learning, a subset of machine learning based on artificial neural networks, is designed to capture complex data patterns through multi-layered structures. By continuously optimizing model performance through iterative learning, it provides a robust and unbiased approach for forecasting and analysis.
- **Target countries:** Eight IPAF member countries (the People's Republic of China [PRC], Indonesia, Kazakhstan, the Republic of Korea [ROK], Malaysia, Mongolia, Thailand, and Viet Nam).
- **Target variable:** Quarterly NPL ratios at the country level for the banking sector unit-based discrepancies from affecting model performance.

Country-level Data	Nominal gross domestic product (GDP), private consumption, government consumption, investment, GDP deflator, total trade of goods and services, gross savings rates, government debt, consolidated fiscal balance, tax revenue, unemployment rate, consumer confidence, consumer price index, producer price index, external debt, nonperforming loans(log), household debt, household mortgage, corporate debt, reserve requirement rate, liquidity assets ratio, capital adequacy ratio, exchange rate against the United States (US) dollar, business confidence, stock market capitalization, industrial production index
Global Data	Global GDP growth, World Bank Total World Unemployment Rate, US Dollar Index, Industrial Production World SA, West Texas Intermediate price, Bloomberg Global-Aggregate Total Return Index

- **Data period:** Available from first quarter (Q1) 2000 to Q3 2024, depending on the country

PRC	'08.4Q~'24.3Q	ROK	'08.3Q~'24.3Q	INO	'12.1Q~'24.3Q	MAL	'13.1Q~'24.3Q
THA	'12.1Q~'24.3Q	VIE	'13.1Q~'24.1Q	MON	'11.1Q~'24.3Q	KAZ	'10.4Q~'23.4Q

PRC = People's Republic of China, INO = Indonesia, KAZ = Kazakhstan, ROK = Republic of Korea, MAL = Malaysia, MON = Mongolia, THA = Thailand, VIE = Viet Nam.

2. Methodology and Data Design

- **Data configuration:** The model is trained using 12 quarters of historical data (training period) to predict the subsequent 4 quarters (forecast horizon). Each dataset thus consists of 16 time series points—12 for input and 4 for output.
- **Training/test split:** In this study, 80% of the configured data windows are used for model training, while the remaining 20% are allocated for validation. To enhance model robustness, the order of the data windows is shuffled. Within each data window, the time series remains sequential, but no specific order is maintained between data windows for training or validation.

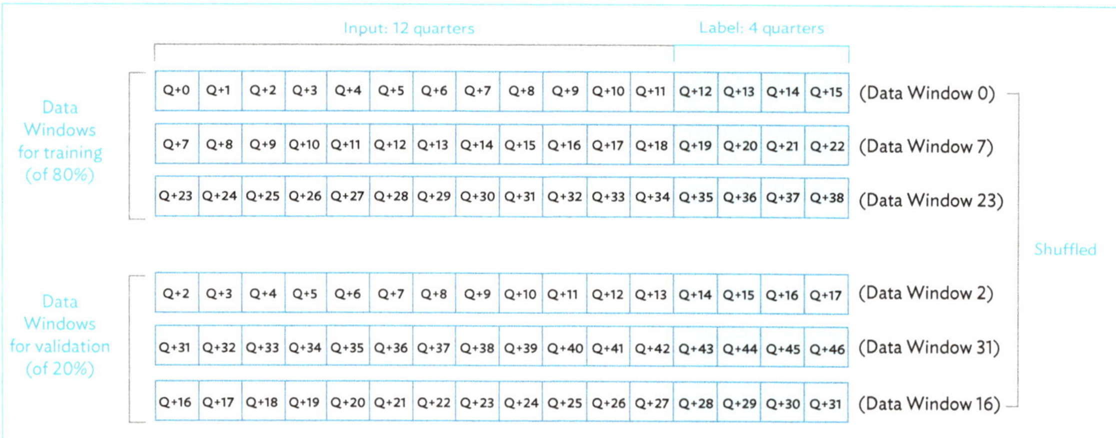

3. Performance Evaluation

- **Model evaluation metric (MAE):** The mean absolute error is used as the performance metric in this study due to its robustness to outliers and its ability to accurately reflect the overall error distribution, making it well-suited for time series forecasting. ※ $MAE = \frac{1}{n}\sum_{i=1}^{n}|y_i - \hat{y}_i|$
- **Validation test results:** The model generally produced estimates close to actual NPL ratios in the training dataset, with MAE remaining within 0.05 percentage points in five countries with relatively accurate predictions.

MAE	PRC	ROK	THA	MAL	INO	VIE	MON	KAZ
(%p)	0.02331	0.02752	0.02530	0.03674	0.04250	0.14591	0.40852	1.07797

4. Empirical Results

- **Summary of Analysis**

NPL Ratio Forecast	PRC Maintain	ROK Slight decline	THA Slight increase	MAL Remain high	INO Sharp increase	VIE Fluctuate	MON More volatile	KAZ Less volatile
Point 1(%)	1.61811	0.39904	2.85094	1.62473	2.56371	3.13954	8.30607	4.23231
Point 2(%)	1.62173	0.37275	2.89028	1.60575	2.72706	3.89628	8.05083	3.83133
Point 3(%)	1.61113	0.37125	2.85842	1.60146	3.07940	2.99632	7.38655	3.64043
Point 4(%)	1.62583	0.35178	2.89965	1.60187	3.11617	3.30976	7.25278	3.35157

PRC = People's Republic of China, INO = Indonesia, KAZ = Kazakhstan, ROK = Republic of Korea, MAL = Malaysia, MON = Mongolia, NPL = nonperforming loan, THA = Thailand, VIE = Viet Nam.

Source: Authors.

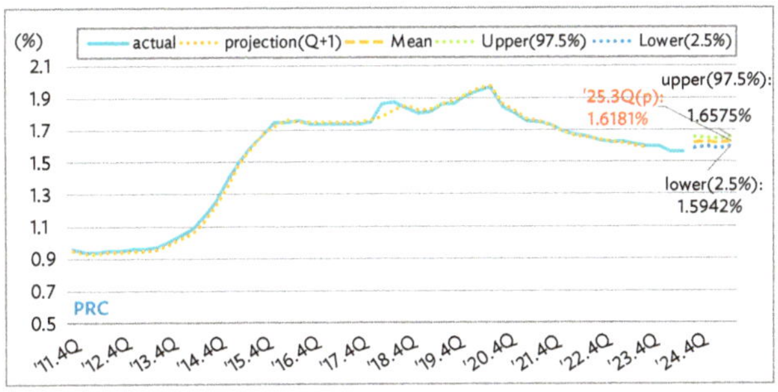

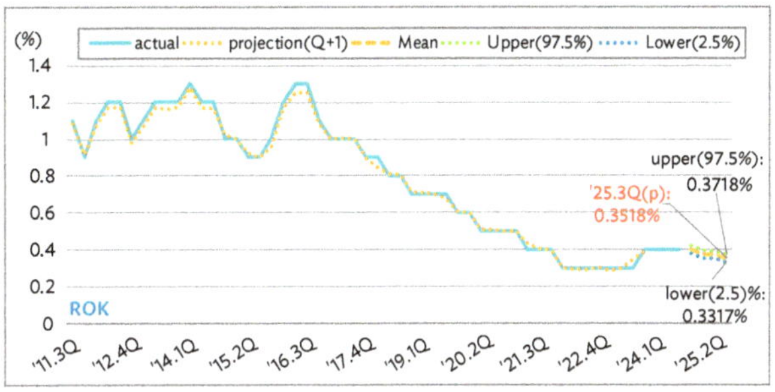

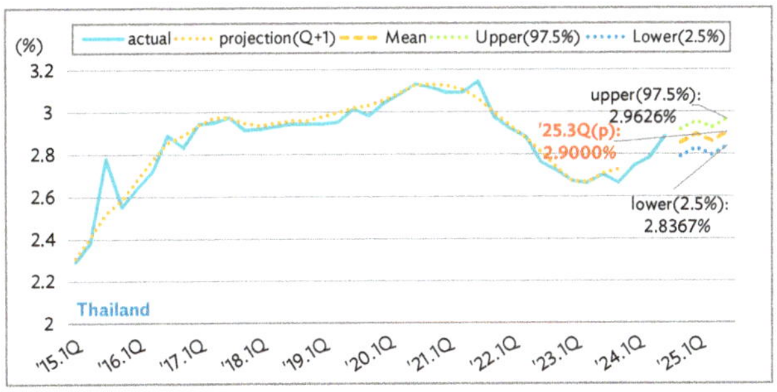

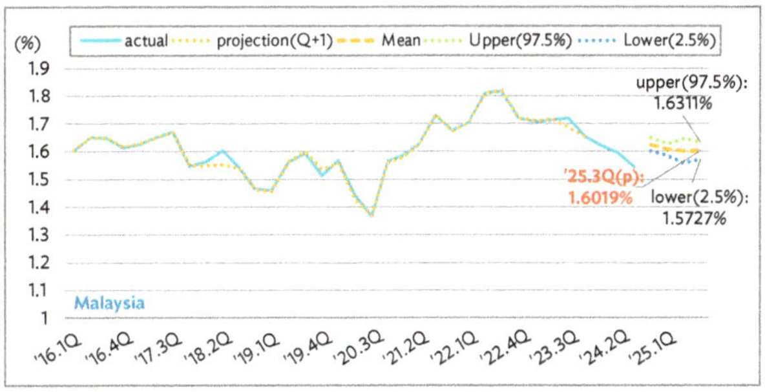

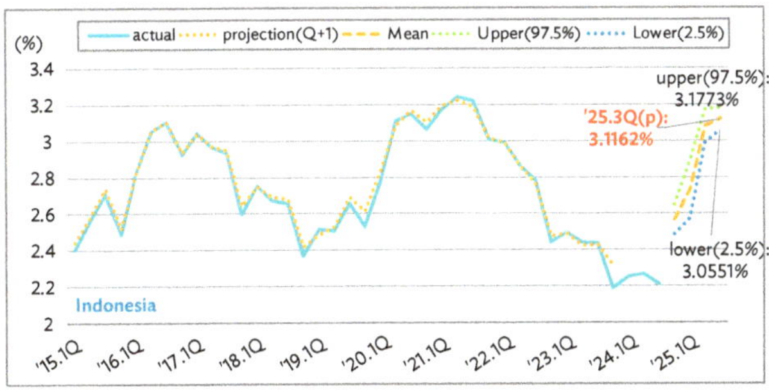

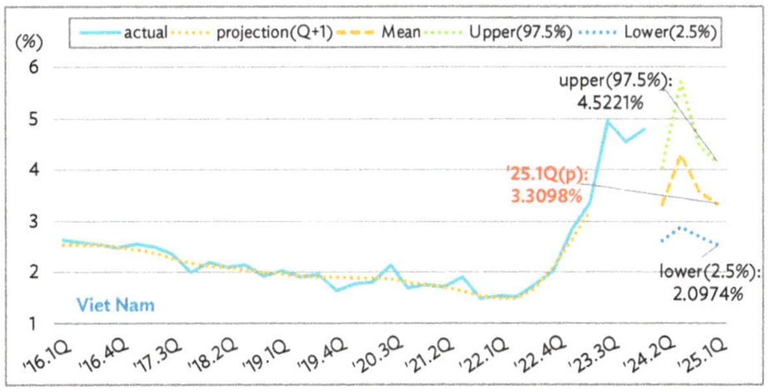

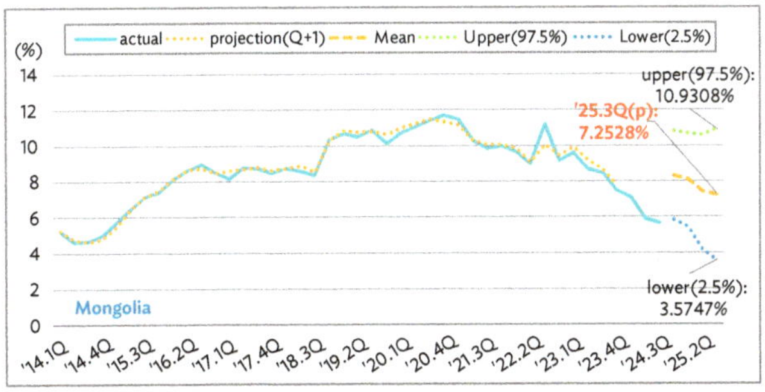

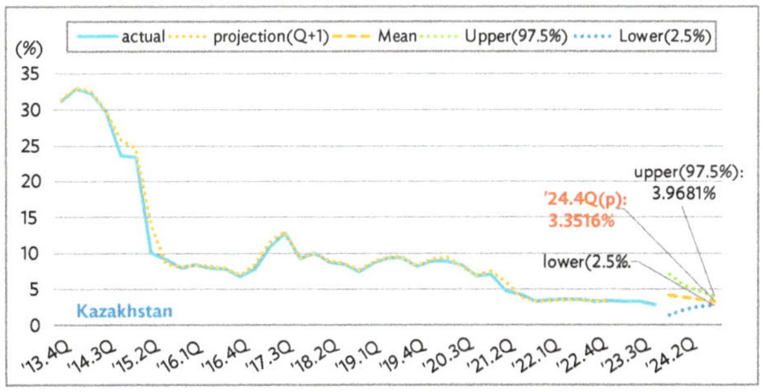

- **PRC, Republic of Korea, Malaysia, and Thailand:** The validation test using the test dataset showed that the model accurately estimated NPL ratios, closely matching actual values during the learning period. As presented in 4. Model Performance (%p) of Table above, the final model achieved an MAE within 0.04 percentage points, demonstrating high estimation accuracy. The forecasts for these four countries closely follow historical trends, and the narrow distribution of results across 1,000 independent simulations indicates stable and reliable predictive performance.
- **Indonesia:** The model forecasts an upward trend in the NPL ratio, diverging notably from its historical patterns. This projected increase was observed consistently across 1,000 simulations, indicating a potential underlying risks. While the black-box nature of deep learning limits direct causal interpretation, several macro-financial factors may help contextualize this trend.
    - Recent studies highlights a contraction in Indonesia's middle class—from 21.45% in 2019 to 17.13% in 2024—largely due to the prolonged effects of the COVID-19 pandemic (Brata 2024). This shift may have weakened household consumption and increased vulnerability of borrowers, particularly in unsecured and SME lending segments. At the same time, a reduced share of middle-income earners may have contributed to slower growth in tax revenues, limiting the government's fiscal space (Rezki et al. 2024). In February 2025, the government announced significant fiscal spending cuts, which could further temper economic momentum and affect credit conditions, especially in sectors reliant on public investments.

      While headline GDP growth remains positive, these developments suggest that income recovery and credit resilience may be uneven factors that could contribute to a gradual rise in NPL ratios, as reflected in the model's forecast.
- **Kazakhstan, Mongolia, and Viet Nam:** These three countries exhibited relatively higher estimation errors compared to other countries in the model, reflecting challenges related to data quality, structural shifts, and historical volatility in NPL ratios. The results underscore the importance of longer time series data and potential model calibration tailored to each country's financial and institutional context.
    - **Kazakhstan** recorded the highest average absolute error during validation. However, forecast variability has narrowed in recent periods, suggesting a more stable credit environment and improved model fit. The NPL ratio has declined markedly since its peak of over 30%, supported by institutional reforms such as the establishment of the FPL in 2012, the adoption of IFRS 9 in 2016, and improved debtor repayment capacity, aided by recovery in global oil prices. These developments may be contributing to more predictable NPL dynamics going forward.
    - **Mongolia** showed substantial NPL fluctuation during the training period, with the ratio ranging from 3.68% in Q2 2013 to a peak of 11.68% in Q4 2020. These swings likely reduced the model's ability to generalize patterns reliably. Since the establishment of MAMCO in 2022, a gradual downward trend in the NPL ratio has been observed. However, forecast variability remains due to lingering structural uncertainty and limited post-reform data
    - **Viet Nam** experienced a notable increase in the NPL ratio beginning in Q4 2021, contributing to greater variability in model forecasts. The relatively limited length of available historical data, especially in the earlier part of the sample, may have constrained the model's ability to fully capture underlying trends, leading to wider confidence intervals and reduced accuracy in later periods.

- **Identify Key Determinants**
    - This section presents the top-15 determinants identified by SHAP for each country. The figure displays the average absolute SHAP values for each feature, where higher values indicate a greater contribution to predictions.

Feature Importance for Future Time Step 1 for the PRC

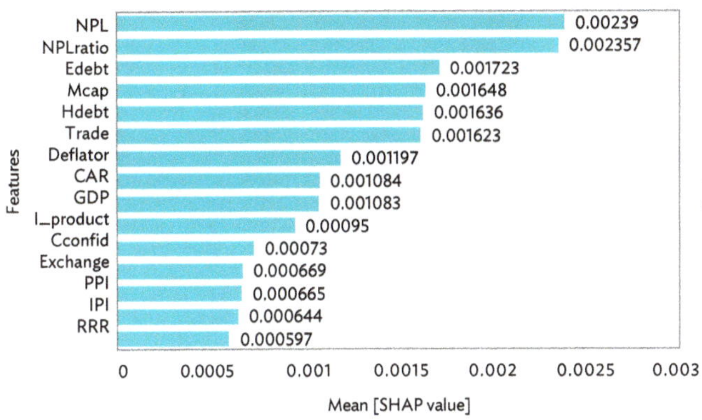

Feature Importance for Future Time Step 1 for Republic of Korea

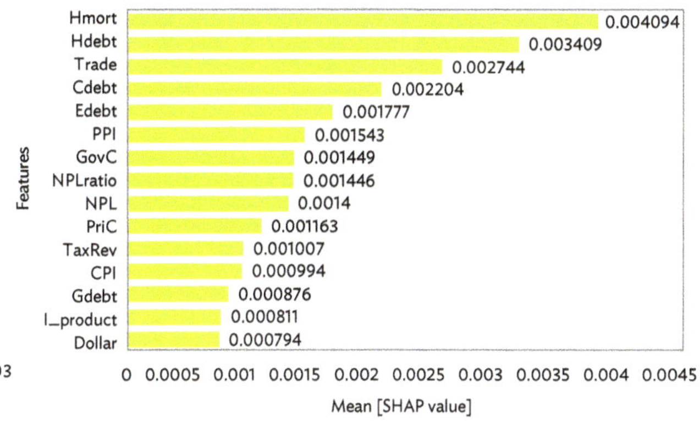

Feature Importance for Future Time Step 1 for Thailand

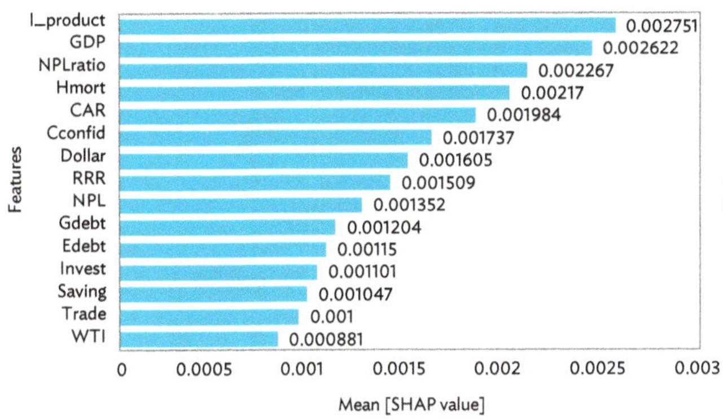

Feature Importance for Future Time Step 1 for Malaysia

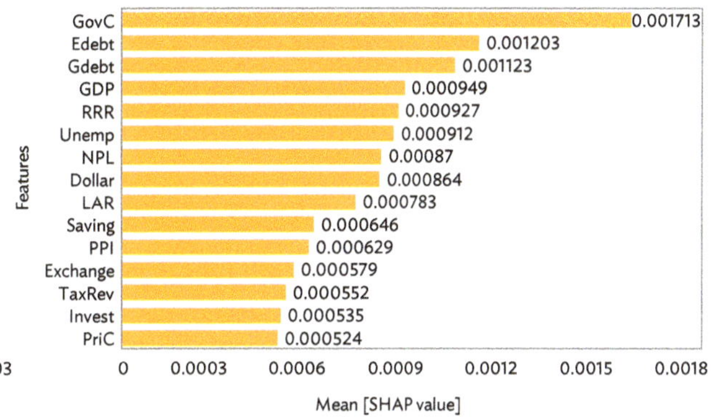

Feature Importance for Future Time Step 1 for Indonesia

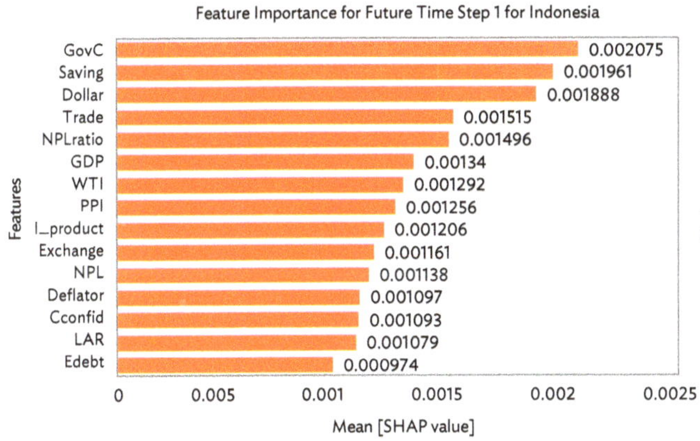

Feature Importance for Future Time Step 1 for Viet Nam

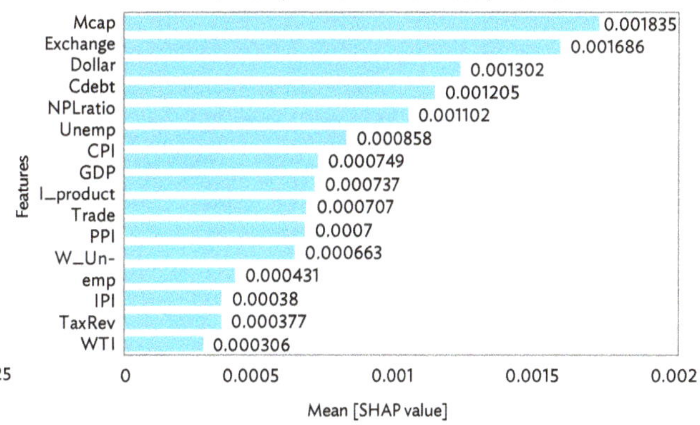

Feature Importance for Future Time Step 1 for Mongolia

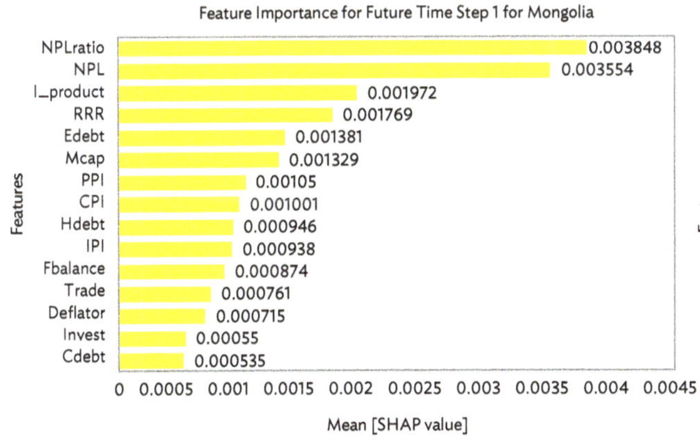

Feature Importance for Future Time Step 1 for Kazakhstan

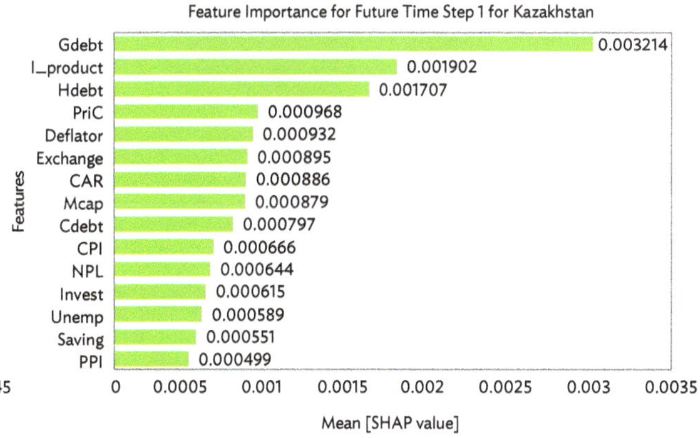

- **PRC and Mongolia:** The past NPL or NPL ratio values were identified as the most influential predictors of future NPL trends, based on SHAP analysis. This reflects a high degree of autocorrelation in NPL dynamics, where historical NPL levels remain a strong signal of near-term outcomes. Such persistence is typical in financial time series, particularly where structural factors or gradual resolution processes delay adjustments in credit quality.
  - In the **PRC**, the strong influence of past NPL ratios may reflect the delayed recognition and resolution of distressed assets, often shaped by policy interventions and regulatory forbearance. This contributes to smoother NPL trajectories over time, reinforcing the predictive power of recent historical values.
  - In **Mongolia**, similar patterns may stem from limited market depth and greater volatility in credit conditions. The slower pace of NPL resolution and structural constraints in the financial system likely contribute to the observed persistence in NPL ratios.
  - While in other Asian countries the influence of past NPL ratios is more modest, their consistent presence among the top determinants supports the value of time series-based modeling approaches, such as LSTM, for capturing these intertemporal dynamics.
- **In the Republic of Korea,** household mortgages and overall household debt were identified as the most influential predictors of future NPL ratio. As of Q4 2024, the household debt-to-GDP ratio is projected to reach 91.7%, the second highest among 38 countries (Institute of International Finance). A large portion of household loans is tied to the housing sector, which has expanded rapidly in recent years. These factors suggest that the NPL outlook in the Republic of Korea may be closely associated with household leverage conditions, particularly in the housing market. The model likely captures the risk that, under adverse conditions such as interest rate hikes or property price corrections, borrower repayment capacity may weaken and affect NPL ratios.
- **In Thailand**, the industrial production index (IPI) appears as the most significant factor influencing future NPL ratio. This may be partly explained by the structure of the Thai economy. Small and medium-sized enterprises (SMEs) make up 99.5% of registered businesses and employ 69.5% of the workforce (World Bank, 2025). Many of these firms operate in industrial and manufacturing sectors and rely on bank financing. CEIC data shows that private nonfinancial sector credit reached 169.4% of GDP as of June 2024, a relatively high level compared to regional peers, such as Indonesia (39%) and Malaysia (134%). These conditions suggest that Thai businesses—particularly SMEs—may be more exposed to shifts in industrial production cycles, with output downturns affecting revenues and repayment capacity. As a result, fluctuations in IPI may offer a forward-looking signal of credit risk in Thailand's banking sector. This may help explain why industrial production features more prominently in Thailand's NPL model compared to countries where household or public-sector dynamics are more dominant.
- **In Indonesia and Malaysia**, government spending emerged as the most influential factor affecting future NPL ratios, according to the SHAP analysis. This result reflects the broader role fiscal policy plays in shaping economic conditions in these countries. Public investment, particularly in infrastructure and social programs, is a key driver of economic activity, supporting sectors such as construction, manufacturing, and services, and contributing to employment and income generation.
  - The model's identification of government spending as a key determinant does not imply a negative judgment on fiscal expansion. Rather, it suggests that the scale and direction of public expenditure may have a meaningful influence on credit dynamics. In periods of increased government spending, the economy may experience stimulus effects that temporarily support borrowers' repayment capacity. Conversely, if spending is reduced or delayed, or if its impact is uneven across sectors, vulnerable borrowers—particularly SMEs reliant on public contracts or downstream demand—may face increased credit risk.

        - In some cases, the efficiency and targeting of fiscal measures may also matter. If public spending is directed toward short-term bailouts or less productive sectors, the temporary relief provided may not translate into sustained improvements in credit quality. Moreover, when fiscal space becomes constrained, a reduction in support programs may expose latent financial stress.
        - Thus, the model's result can be interpreted as highlighting the importance of fiscal policy as a macroeconomic transmission channel—rather than suggesting that spending itself is a direct cause of NPL growth. The influence of government expenditure on NPL trends may reflect its indirect effects on aggregate demand, firm performance, and employment conditions in both economies.
    - **In Kazakhstan**, government debt was identified as the most influential factor associated with future NPL ratios. This may reflect the historical interaction between public sector support and banking sector stability. Between 2009 and 2023, the government implemented at least 24 fiscal measures in response to banking sector stress, including direct support to individual banks. Notably, in 2017, the recapitalization of Kazkommertsbank alone amounted to 7.2% of GDP and 44% of total government revenue. These interventions suggest that changes in public debt levels often coincide with periods of elevated NPLs. In this context, government debt may serve as a proxy for broader financial system risks or underlying credit challenges that prompt state intervention. The model may be capturing this association between sovereign liabilities and banking sector conditions, particularly in settings where public intervention plays a recurring role in NPL resolution.
    - **In Viet Nam**, stock market capitalization was identified as a key factor influencing NPL ratio forecasts. While this relationship is not commonly observed in other economies in the sample, it may be linked to structural features of Viet Nam's financial system. As of October 2024, foreign ownership in several major Vietnamese banks exceeded 20%, including Viet Nam Prosperity JSC Bank (27.8%), Viet Nam JSC Bank for Industry and Trade (27.1%), and JSC Bank for Foreign Trade of Viet Nam (23.4%). This level of participation may indicate a closer link between banking sector conditions and equity market developments.
        - One possible interpretation is that stock market capitalization reflects shifts in financial conditions or investor sentiment, which may influence credit growth and risk-taking behavior. In periods of strong market performance, credit expansion may increase, while downturns could coincide with tighter financial conditions. In this context, stock market capitalization may serve as an indirect indicator of the broader financial environment, which could be relevant to NPL dynamics. Further analysis may be needed to better understand the transmission channel between market indicators and credit risk in this case.

7. Conclusion and Policy Implications

This study applied deep learning techniques to forecast NPL ratios and identify key macro-financial determinants across eight IPAF member countries. The two-layer LSTM model, selected for its superior forecasting performance, demonstrated high accuracy in countries with stable and extensive datasets. The integration of SHAP values allowed for interpretability of the model outputs, offering country-specific insights into the variables most influencing NPL trends.

The findings confirm that NPL drivers vary significantly across economies: household debt and mortgages dominate in the Republic of Korea, industrial production in Thailand, government spending in Indonesia and Malaysia, government debt in Kazakhstan, and stock market capitalization in Viet Nam. In the PRC and Mongolia, past NPL values themselves were the strongest predictors, highlighting strong autocorrelation.

These country-level distinctions emphasize the importance of tailored policy responses. Policymakers should focus on improving data consistency and length, especially in countries with high model variability, such as Mongolia and Viet Nam. Deep learning can support early warning systems and financial surveillance, but its success relies on the quality of input data.

From a regional cooperation perspective, these insights offer valuable opportunities for IPAF members to share knowledge and practices related to credit risk monitoring, fiscal interventions, and structural reforms. Strengthening cross-border dialogue and building a shared platform for data and predictive modeling could significantly enhance the region's financial resilience.

Annex 6: 2024 People's Republic of China Nonperforming Loans Markets and Index Reports

Released by ZSAMC Research Institute *(As of May 2025)*

The 2024 People's Republic of China (PRC) NPL Market Report provides a comprehensive overview of the asset quality trends, transaction dynamics, and judicial auction developments in the PRC. The NPL ratio remained stable at 1.59% in early 2024 and slightly decreased by year-end, with the total NPL balance declining to CNY 3.28 trillion.

Primary market NPL transaction volume dropped by 23% year-on-year to CNY301.7 billion, with joint-stock and city commercial banks as major contributors. The big five AMCs (CITIC, Cinda, Orient, Great Wall, Galaxy) dominated both the buying (59.2%) and selling (62.7%) sides of the primary market. In the secondary market, transaction volume also contracted by 37.8%, with non-AMC investors acquiring 84% of the assets—indicating a more price-sensitive and competitive environment.

Online NPL auctions saw over 10,000 cases, mostly involving small-sized loans under CNY10 million. Guangdong and Jiangsu were the most active provinces, and the national average discount rate was about 48%. Though representing a smaller segment of the overall market, online auction pricing trends still reflected broader macroeconomic influences.

The personal NPL market expanded rapidly in 2024, driven by regulatory pilot programs and year-end balance sheet management by financial institutions. Transaction volume surged 64% year-on-year to CNY158.35 billion, with Ping An Bank and provincial AMCs leading the activity. The average discount rate on personal NPL portfolios remained under 3%, with recovery rates around 8.5%.

Collateral judicial auctions increased sharply, especially in Zhejiang (up 61.9%) and Guangdong (up 95.8%). However, auction liquidity weakened, requiring more cycles to close deals. Discount rates for residential, commercial, and industrial collateral all declined, reflecting cautious buyer sentiment amid economic uncertainty.

Overall, the 2024 NPL market in the PRC showed signs of cautious optimism, marked by continued asset quality improvements, active regulatory oversight, and evolving investor behavior in both traditional and online channels.

Bibliography

Asian Development Bank (ADB). 2021. *Nonperforming Loans in Asia and Europe—Causes, Impacts, and Resolution Strategies.* ADB. https://www.adb.org/publications/nonperforming-loans-asia-europe-causes-impacts.

———. 2022. Road Map for Developing an Online Platform to Trade Nonperforming Loans in Asia and the Pacific. October. https://www.adb.org/sites/default/files/publication/832521/road-map-online-platform-trade-nonperforming-loans.pdf.

———. 2024a. *How to Build Nonperforming Loan Trading Platforms in Asia and the Pacific*. ADB. https://www.adb.org/sites/default/files/publication/969886/nonperforming-loan-platforms-asia-pacific.pdf.

———. 2024b. IPAF 2024 Training Materials on Digital Platform Design and Legal Harmonisation. April.

———. 2025. *Asian Development Outlook April 2025.* https://www.adb.org/outlook/editions/april-2025.

ASEAN+3 Macroeconomic Research Office (AMRO). 2024. *ASEAN+3 Financial Stability Report 2024*. AMRO. https://amro-asia.org/asean3-financial-stability-report-2024/.

European Bank for Reconstruction and Development. 2024. NPL Monitor H2 2024. https://npl.vienna-initiative.com/assets/Uploads/2024/NPL-Monitor-H2-2024-fv.pdf.

Fitch Ratings. 2024. What Investors Want to Know: APAC Banks' Risk Appetite and Asset Quality. https://www.fitchratings.com/research/banks/what-investors-want-to-know-apac-banks-risk-appetite-asset-quality-09-12-2024.

———. 2025. APAC Investors See Broadly Favourable Financing Conditions in 2025. *Fitch Wire.* 27 January. https://www.fitchratings.com/research/banks/apac-investors-see-broadly-favourable-financing-conditions-in-2025-27-01-2025.

International Finance Corporation. 2025. Viet Nam: Creating Pre-Conditions for a Nonperforming Loan Market. January. https://www.ifc.org/content/dam/ifc/doclink/2025/gfip-case-studies-vietnam-jan2025pdf.pdf.

International Monetary Fund (IMF). 2024a. Global Financial Stability Report: Safeguarding Financial Stability amid High Debt and Tightening Conditions. April. https://www.imf.org/en/Publications/GFSR/Issues/2024/04/10/global-financial-stability-report-april-2024.

———. 2024b. People's Republic of China: 2024 Article IV Consultation-Press Release. https://www.elibrary.imf.org/view/journals/002/2024/258/002.2024.issue-258-en.pdf.

———. 2024c. *Regional Economic Outlook for Asia and Pacific, November 2024*. IMF. https://www.imf.org/en/Publications/REO/APAC/Issues/2024/10/31/regional-economic-outlook-for-asia-and-pacific-october-2024.

———. 2024d. *The Case for (and Against) Asset Management Companies in Banking Crises*. IMF. https://www.imf.org/-/media/Files/Publications/TNM/2024/English/TNMEA2024004.ashx.

———. 2024e. *World Economic Outlook, April 2024*. Chapter 1: Global Prospects and Policies. https://www.imf.org/-/media/Files/Publications/WEO/2024/April/English/ch1.ashx.

International Public Asset Management Companies Forum (IPAF). 2024a. Data Requirements for Trading and Valuing NPLs & Blueprint for NPL Online Trading Platforms. April. https://ipafasia.org/uploads/events/training-indonesia-2024/Session-2C_NPL_Transaction_Platforms_in_8th_IPAF_Training_2024.pdf.

———. 2024b. 8th IPAF Training Seminar, Jakarta 2024. https://ipafasia.org/activities/training%26aid%3D27%26title%3D8th-ipaf-training-seminar-jakarta-2024.

Korea Asset Management Corporation (KAMCO). 2021. History – Corporate Overview. https://www.kamco.or.kr/eng/contents.do?mId=0102020000.

Moody's Analytics. 2024. NPL Risk Trends in Asia: Rising Pressure in Mid-Tier Lenders. Moody's Risk Perspectives, February.

Nikkei Asia. 2024. Asian Banks Bracing for Higher NPLs in 2024 as Rate Pressures Persist. 21 February.

Reuters. 2024a. ADB Maintains Growth Forecast for Developing Asia, Says More Stimulus Expected in China. 25 September. https://www.reuters.com/markets/asia/adb-maintains-growth-forecast-developing-asia-says-more-stimulus-expected-china-2024-09-25.

———. 2024b. China Banks Brace for Tide of Bad Property Loans. 15 April. https://www.spglobal.com/ratings/en/research/articles/240415-china-banks-brace-for-tide-of-bad-property-loans-13068811 .

———. 2024c. China Bohai Seeks to Dispose of $4 Billion in Bad Loans. 22 July. https://www.reuters.com/business/finance/stanchart-linked-china-bohai-seeks-dispose-4-bln-bad-loans-2024-07-22/.

———. 2024d. China's Banks Have a Nasty Case of Indigestion. 10 September. https://www.reuters.com/breakingviews/chinas-banks-have-nasty-case-indigestion-2024-09-10/.

———. 2024e. HSBC Hit by Sixfold Surge in Hong Kong Property Loan Defaults. August. https://www.ft.com/content/09824227-8959-4ed2-a1ba-a7c7f6b27e4a.

———. 2024f. Indonesia Gives Small, Medium Businesses Six-Month Window for Loan Forgiveness. 11 November. https://www.reuters.com/markets/asia/indonesia-gives-small-medium-businesses-six-month-window-loan-forgiveness-2024-11-11.

———. 2025a. Asia Credit Starts to Wobble as Market Pain Spreads. 7 April. https://www.reuters.com/markets/asia/asia-credit-starts-wobble-market-pain-spreads-2025-04-07/.

———. 2025b. Bank Indonesia to Hold Rates on April 23 as FX Concerns Outweigh Growth Risks: Reuters Poll. 21 April. https://www.reuters.com/markets/asia/bank-indonesia-hold-rates-april-23-fx-concerns-outweigh-growth-risks-2025-04-21.

———. 2025c. China's March Bank Loans Seen Rebounding as Trade Tensions Escalate. 9 April. https://www.reuters.com/markets/asia/chinas-march-bank-loans-seen-rebounding-trade-tensions-escalate-2025-04-09/.

———. 2025d. China's Banks Hike Consumer Loan Rates in Abrupt Reversal as Bad Debt Risks Mount. 1 April. https://www.reuters.com/world/china/chinese-banks-hike-consumer-loan-rates-abrupt-reversal-bad-debt-risks-mount-2025-04-01/.

———. 2025e. India Moves to Deepen Junk Debt Market by Allowing Bad Loan Securitisation. 15 April. https://www.reuters.com/world/india/india-moves-deepen-junk-debt-market-by-allowing-bad-loan-securitisation-2025-04-15.

———. 2025f. India Private Banks See Higher Levels of Small Loan Defaults until Mid-2025. 10 February. https://www.reuters.com/world/india/india-private-banks-see-higher-levels-small-loan-defaults-until-mid-2025-2025-02-10.

———. 2025g. S.Korea Signals Rate Cuts in May, Year Ahead as Trump Tariffs Pose 'Significant' Risks. 17 April. https://www.reuters.com/markets/rates-bonds/south-korea-holds-rates-trump-tariffs-heighten-economic-risks-2025-04-17/.

———. 2025h. Signs of Rising Asset Quality Stress Spook Indian Bank Stocks. 20 January. https://www.reuters.com/business/finance/signs-rising-asset-quality-stress-spook-indian-bank-stocks-2025-01-20/.

———. 2025i. Thailand Approves Support Measures for Non-Bank Debtors. 11 February. https://www.reuters.com/markets/asia/thailand-approves-support-measures-non-bank-debtors-2025-02-11.

———. 2025j. Viet Nam to Finalise Restructuring Plan for Troubled Lender SCB, State Media Says. 21 April. https://money.usnews.com/investing/news/articles/2025-04-21/vietnam-central-bank-preparing-restructuring-plan-for-troubled-lender-scb#:~:text=HANOI%20%28Reuters%29%20-%20Vietnam%27s%20central%20bank%20is%20finalising,biggest%20financial%20fraud%20on%20record%2C%20local%20media%20reported.

S&P Global Ratings. 2024a. Asia-Pacific Financial Institutions Monitor 1Q 2024: Property Exposures Will Chart the Course. 7 February. https://www.spglobal.com/ratings/en/research/articles/240207-asia-pacific-financial-institutions-monitor-1q-2024-property-exposures-will-chart-the-course-12994261.

———. 2024b. China Banks' Property NPLs to Peak at RMB 660 Billion in 2024. https://www.spglobal.com/ratings/en/research/articles/230420-china-banks-property-npls-to-peak-at-rmb660-billion-in-2024-12702152.

———. 2025c. Asia-Pacific Corporates 2025: Who Can Take the Tariff Hit? https://www.spglobal.com/_assets/documents/ratings/research/101617088.pdf.

———. 2025d. Asia-Pacific Economies Likely to Be Hit by U.S. Trade Tariffs. https://www.spglobal.com/ratings/en/research/articles/250224-economic-research-asia-pacific-economies-likely-to-be-hit-by-u-s-trade-tariffs-13421482.

———. 2025c. Credit Conditions Asia-Pacific Q1 2025: Bracing for Volatility. January. https://www.spglobal.com/_assets/documents/ratings/research/101609703.pdf.

———. 2025d. Credit Cycle Indicator Q2 2025: Macro Headwinds Could Hinder Credit Recovery. https://www.spglobal.com/_assets/documents/ratings/research/101618052.pdf.

Statista. 2024a. South Korea: Coverage Ratio of Non-Performing Bank Loans 2024. https://www.statista.com/statistics/1242111/south-korea-coverage-ratio-of-non-performing-bank-loans/.

———. 2024b. China: Non-Performing Loan Stock 2024. September. https://www.statista.com/statistics/1171742/china-non-performing-loan-stock/.

UBS Asset Management. 2025. Asia Credit Market on the Recovery Path. February. https://www.ubs.com/global/en/assetmanagement/insights/asset-class-perspectives/fixed-income/articles/asia-credit-market-recovery.html.

Viet Nam Debt and Asset Trading Corporation (DATC). 2024. International Cooperation Activities.

Vietnam News. 2025. Banking Industry to Focus on Bad Debt Handling Targets in 2025. 3 January. https://vietnamnews.vn/economy/1689996/banking-industry-to-focus-on-bad-debt-handling-targets-in-2025.html.

World Bank. 2024a. Pakistan Development Update. April. https://thedocs.worldbank.org/en/doc/140b30353b40dbb294cca42bcb86529a-0310062024/original/Pakistan-Development-Update-April-2024.pdf.

———. 2024b. Commodity Markets Outlook. October. https://openknowledge.worldbank.org/server/api/core/bitstreams/bbda9ad3-4f12-4626-ad4b-94a4d20fbd52/content.

ZSAMC. 2025. 2024 China NPL Market Report. https://ipafasia.org/uploads/newsletter/2024-China-NPL-Market-Report.pdf.

www.ingramcontent.com/pod-product-compliance
Lightning Source LLC
Chambersburg PA
CBHW041758220926
51847CB00014B/244
* 9 7 8 9 2 9 2 7 7 3 9 6 0 *